William Bright

Bright's single Stem, Dwarf and renewal System of Grape Culture

Adapted to the Vineyard, the Grapery, and the fruiting of Vines in Pots, on Trellises, Arbors, etc.

William Bright

Bright's single Stem, Dwarf and renewal System of Grape Culture
Adapted to the Vineyard, the Grapery, and the fruiting of Vines in Pots, on Trellises, Arbors, etc.

ISBN/EAN: 9783337183660

Printed in Europe, USA, Canada, Australia, Japan

Cover: Foto ©Andreas Hilbeck / pixelio.de

More available books at **www.hansebooks.com**

BRIGHT'S

SINGLE STEM, DWARF AND RENEWAL

SYSTEM OF

GRAPE CULTURE,

ADAPTED TO THE VINEYARD, THE GRAPERY, AND THE FRUITING OF VINES IN POTS, ON TRELLISES, ARBORS, ETC.

"Things which bring in money, will be sure to make their own way."
—*Leibig on Modern Agriculture.*

BY WILLIAM BRIGHT,

Logan Nursery, Philadelphia.

PHILADELPHIA:
PUBLISHED BY THE AUTHOR.
NEW YORK:
C. M. SAXTON, BARKER & CO.
1860.

Bright on Grape Culture.

The Single Stem, Dwarf and Renewal System of Grape Culture.

WE presume every grape-grower has felt the want of some simple, definite and efficient system of managing the vine, especially in the vineyard, and upon small arbors and trellises. After all the talk about grape culture, no one that we know of has any established method of pruning and training the vine, which may be pronounced a simple, complete and satisfactory system. The German method, as practised at Cincinnati, it is admitted, is not well adapted to the production of perfect table grapes; and the Thomery system, advocated by Dr. C. W. Grant, though elegant and successful on high trellises, is not adapted to vines with long joints, nor to general vineyard culture. To allow vines to range almost unrestrained over tall trees and immense arbors, is by many considered the perfection of wisdom, while it is literally a great system with no system at all.

All vines running to a great height, must of necessity have an immense length of barren cane in proportion to its fruiting wood, and this barrenness is yearly increasing. The best qualities of our native grapes, we feel convinced, can never be developed, unless a better method of pruning and training be adopted by grape growers; and with the hope of aiding the accomplishment of this object, we here present our system of culture, which, if not the best that can be devised, is, we believe, far superior to any system at present in use in the United States.

The "dwarf and renewal system," as we style it, though not entirely original with the writer, is the result of long experience in the culture of the vine, and embodies some methods of managing the grape, of great value, which are not generally known or practised by other cultivators.

The writer believes that his system is beyond all question the best that can be adopted for grape culture, in America, in all cases. It is, in the main, *a method of fruiting the vine on a single, short cane, with very short lateral branches,*—growing new wood from the main stem one year, and fruiting it the next; dwarfing the vine by a definite rule of stopping and pruning, and renewing the entire wood of the vine, (except a small portion of the main stem,) every other year.

This system possesses many important advantages over any other method of culture, which will become apparent after proper examination or trial.

Its chief merit is, that it concentrates the entire strength of the vine roots upon a small quantity of young, vigorous wood, and produces larger and finer bunches of grapes than can be obtained by any other process. As to quantity of crop, it is equal, if not superior, to any other system of culture. Indeed, it is believed, that in the vineyard or elsewhere, this system will produce a larger crop of grapes than can be obtained from the same extent of soil upon long canes, under any of the ordinary methods of pruning.

The vines grown according to this system are more perfectly under control than when allowed to ramble over long ranges of wire or trellises; they are more easily trained and tied up, or laid down in winter; they can be kept in a more healthy and vigorous condition; and when they decline in health or fruiting capacity, any entire vine may be readily renewed by layering, thus producing a new set of roots near the surface of the ground, without essentially interfering with the general product of the vineyard.

The common idea is, that the Isabella, Catawba, and other native American vines, must be allowed to ramble almost at will; it is contended that their wild, natural character demands this treatment, and that any attempt to cut them back severely, will injure their health and fruitfulness. This idea may be correct, as applied to any of the common methods of pruning, but it is not correct when considered in relation to the method of culture advocated in this work. It may be improper to prune severely an old vine, with a long cane, but such is not our system. We grow an entire vine one season, and fruit it the next; we do not cut back severely an old vine already grown. The vine under this system is allowed to expend its whole strength, wild rambling nature and all, during one season, in the production of a new and perfect cane; the next season it is permitted to produce a full crop of fruit, as full and as heavy as its wood and roots are able to perfect. If this is not work enough for the roots, as much work, in fact, as any vine is called upon to perform, then we have made a great mistake in our estimate of the matter.

The opponents of dwarf culture declare that this system may answer for foreign grapes in pots, but will not answer for the Isabella, and other hardy native grapes; this opinion being based upon the idea that the native grapes, with their wild character, are more free in growth than the foreign vines. But this latter opinion is positively incorrect. It is not true that the native grapes are more vigorous or free in growth than the foreign kinds, as every grape-grower, who has ever cultivated the foreign kinds under glass, must admit. The whole theory upon which the dwarf culture of native grapes is opposed, is founded in error. The foreign vines are in fact vastly more free in growth, more wild, if you please, than the Isabella, or any other native; yet the foreign vines endure the dwarfing process in pot culture, not only without injury, but with the highest degree of success. The same is true of the Isabella and other native vines. We have tried them in pots, on arbors and trellises, and in the vineyard, on our system, and have found the fears of grape-growers, as to the injurious effects of dwarfing, entirely without foundation.

Upon our system, in fact, the free flow of sap from the roots is not checked or restrained; it finds full and free outlet in the formation of wood, foliage and fruit, —as full and free as if permitted to run to the terminal points of a vine fifty feet long. We give the roots work enough to do, and they are never "made sick with excess of sap," as it is feared they may be, when the idea of dwarf culture is suggested. We know, by experience, the best of teachers, that what we say is true; and we can show the evidence of our knowledge and experience, in thrifty vines and large crops of the finest bunches of native grapes, grown upon the dwarf renewal system, in the season of fruit, to any one who may choose to examine them.

The truth is, that our dwarf renewal system of vine culture is perfectly adapted to native grapes, as well as to the foreign kinds; it most perfectly meets the wants of grape-growers in the United States, in graperies and vineyards, and on arbors and trellises; and will afford every person who practises it, the highest amount of pleasure and profit.

We have purposely described the system of pruning, here advocated, in *detail*, in several sections of this work, as adapted to the cold grapery, vineyard, &c., preferring to make some repetition, rather than to fail of being understood by readers of different classes, who may wish to employ this system in the various kinds of culture.

The method of "stopping," which we have prescribed, is peculiarly our own, being the result of our personal experience and practice in pot vine culture; and the detached and divided border for the vinery, is also quite original with us. We believe that we have been the first to publish any suggestion of such a border, and the first to construct a house on this plan.

We also advocate, more strictly and emphatically than any other writer that we know of, shallow and moderately rich borders, very shallow planting, surface manuring and heavy mulching, as necessary to success in grape culture.

The *alternate renewal plan*, which we recommend, has never before, we believe, been presented to the public, or practised in the vineyard, as a distinct and definite system, and may therefore be claimed as original.

Our method of top-dressing and manuring, and the combination of fertilizers employed, are, we believe, in many respects new; and we feel assured that they are based upon scientific principles, which will bear the test of investigation and practical trial.

This work was originally intended to be simply a hand-book of instruction in the management of the grape vine in pots, and the system we advocate has chiefly grown out of our experience in that kind of culture; we shall therefore first treat of the propagation and fruiting of vine in pots. What follows, on the vineyard and grapery, we have been induced to add at the earnest request of several friends, who think as we do, that our system is well adapted to general use, and ought to be made public. We feel well assured that no one who may try this method of pruning will have any cause to regret it.

Culture of the Grape Vine in Pots.

The art of growing and fruiting the grape vine in pots, forms one of the most interesting, elegant, and profitable branches of modern horticulture. When well understood, the culture of the vine in this way will be found to be as simple and as easy as in the border, and even better suited to the circumstances and wants of numerous amateurs and gardeners.

Anybody who has a small forcing-house, may produce the best foreign grapes in pots in perfection, without the costly preparations of the vinery, and with very little trouble. If the grape, when fruited, is an elegant object in the vinery, it is much more so in the pot; and when managed with skill, the mass of splendid fruit which a single cane less than three feet in height is capable of producing, cannot fail to excite the admiration of every beholder.

A great many persons who have small green-houses, would like to raise grapes. To such, pot-culture offers peculiar advantages. The work of growing the vines can be easily and cheaply done by themselves or their gardeners, and the plants got ready in any number, (as will be hereafter described,) and brought forward, say a dozen or two at a time, without interfering with the other plants, and fruited as soon as in a regular hothouse, and in great abundance and perfection.

For early forcing, the pot vine is exceedingly convenient. The owner of a vinery may desire a few early grapes, but it may be impossible or undesirable to heat the border early in the season, and go into general forcing. In such cases, with the control easily exercised over the pot vines, we may start them in the hothouse in the month of March, and after the fruit is set, ripen in the cold vinery, and cut the fruit in June or July.

There is great economy of space in pot-culture, which commends it especially to persons who have hot-houses of limited extent. Five hundred square feet of glass will ripen about two hundred and fifty pounds of grapes, in a common house, with border culture. In pots, five hundred pounds, at least, may be obtained under the same surface of glass, and the period of ripening may be more easily hastened or retarded; thus in a single house greatly extending the fruit season.

Grapes in pots may also be kept for three or four months upon the vines, after they are ripened, by removing the pots to a cool, dry, airy room—even in the parlor—thus presenting all the merit of a beautiful house plant, as an object of interest, as well as a delicious source of gratification to the palate. West's St. Peter's, Muscat, and several other late grapes, ripened in pots on the 1st of October, will keep on the vines, in a cool, dry, airy room, till the 1st of February or March.

As an ornament to the dinner table, or for decorating a room for evening parties, there is no production of the hot-house more truly magnificent in all respects, than a pot vine fully and properly developed, bearing six or seven bunches of the finest grapes, as they may be grown by proper dwarf culture, such as we shall describe in this work.

The early fruiting of dwarf pot vines is another advantage greatly in their favor, as compared with common vines. Vines are so easily produced in pots, that it is a matter of little consideration if you fruit them early, at the expense of the existence of the vine, while in the border you would be more careful to create a strong cane before permitting it to fruit. Vines may be struck from the eye, and forced into perfect and abundant fruiting in eighteen months. You may strike vines from the eye in March, and fruit them in pots the second season, moderately, without serious injury to them.

Properly and moderately fruited, the pot vine is not destroyed, as many persons suppose, in one or two seasons, but may be shifted from small to larger pots, root-pruned, and again placed in smaller pots, for years, the proper nutriment for growing wood and perfecting fruit being added to the soil at each change of pots, and given in solution while bearing. A much greater *variety* of grapes may be grown together in pots in the same house, than by the common method in borders. When the roots of vines run together, it is well known that the strong-growing sorts are apt to injure and drive out the weaker kinds, as for instance, the strong-growing White Nice, Syrian, or Buel, planted in a border by the side of the Black Prince, or the Dutch Sweet Water, will so seriously check the growth of the latter, that perfect fruiting is almost impossible. With vines in pots no such accident can happen. Each plant is perfectly independent of every other, and they may be placed side by side without injury.

It will be here understood that we are speaking of true and exclusive pot vine culture—not that partial or mixed system which permits the roots of the vine to extend from the pots into a border.

In pot culture, grapes which it is impossible to ripen in the border without cracking, may be produced in the utmost perfection. The Chasselas Musque is a grape of this description. The cracking is due to excess of moisture in the border, which it is sometimes difficult to prevent. But in the pot we have entire control over the moisture, and hence perfect grapes can be produced.

A question which almost every man will ask, in respect to pot vine culture, is this: "Will it pay?" We answer, most unhesitatingly, it will. We know it will pay. We grant that pot vines require more care and attention than vines in borders; but they may be employed by many persons who have only small hothouses, without interfering with other plants, and without any great additional expense; large crops of early grapes (and late ones too,) may be obtained where none could otherwise be grown; and the return, for the space occupied and care required, in pecuniary profit and personal gratification, will be found highly satisfactory.

Growing foreign grapes in hothouses is generally considered a sort of rich man's luxury. The pot vine may, on the contrary, be called the poor man's luxury. The grape in borders is generally grown on a man's own estate. The pot vine may be called the tenant's grape. In pots, the grape may be grown in any sort of hothouse, even in a three-light box, by the tenant of the humblest cottage; and when he is suddenly called upon, by any circumstance, to remove, he may take his vine with him, at any season of the year, and continue its culture at his pleasure.

There are many persons who have much taste for horticultural pursuits, and for the culture of grapes in particular, not restricted in means, who yet do not find it desirable to erect permanent graperies. To such, as well as to the really poor man, the pot vine is a most desirable acquisition. In city yards, where a greenhouse only ten feet square can be erected, there the grape may be grown and fruited in pots as perfectly as in the most costly and extensive structures.

With these advantages of pot vine culture before us, we think we may safely say, that when the art of growing and fruiting the grape in this way becomes fully and generally known, it will be exceedingly popular.

It is an art which ladies may learn and exercise under circumstances well suited to their tastes, and may even be made a source of profit, as well as pleasure, by many ladies who would not choose to engage in any common gainful occupation. To the man of wealth, who has extensive hot-houses, it will add to his vines a convenient method of early forcing, and an elegant novelty for the parlor or the supper-party; and to the person of more limited means, it affords an opportunity to enjoy the pleasure of growing the richest grapes, at small expense, in the highest perfection.

Propagation and Culture of Pot Vines.

STRIKING FROM EYES, AND POTTING.

To strike from eyes, select good, strong, well ripened wood—the stronger the better—as soon as the vines are pruned. Be careful not to let the wood become dry. Place the wood in a cool spot, and cover it with damp soil or sand. About the first of March, bed each eye in plain bar sand, in a shallow box, at an angle of about 45°, so as to leave the eye slightly projecting. Keep the sand moderately moist, and place the box containing it in a bottom heat of about 80°, and under a solar heat of about 50° to 55°. The eyes will begin to break in about a month. Pot off in four inch pots, with equal portions of leaf mould, sand and loam. Plunge the pots back into the same bottom heat, increasing the solar heat to 65°; and water copiously when the plant is becoming established.

SHIFTING POTS.

As soon as the pot becomes well filled with roots, say in four weeks, shift the vines to seven inch pots.

In the preparation of the soil for these pots, there is an opportunity for the exercise of much scientific skill. The common method is, to make a compost of old sod, and a little well rotted stable manure, with the addition of a small quantity of finely ground bones. The leading requirements of the vine, *for the formation of roots and wood*, are carbonaceous loam, alkaline phosphates, silicate of potash, carbonate of soda and lime, and a good proportion of nitrogenous manure. Our method of making composts for vine borders, so as to combine the requisite ingredients in the proper proportions, will be given in another part of this work.

Proper drainage must of course be provided in the pot. Pack the soil firmly about the roots, and give water moderately till the pot becomes well filled with roots, then water copiously. About the middle of May remove the pots to the vinery, and treat them as you would any ordinary vine. Remember that the vine is a gross feeder, and requires an abundant supply of water in sunny weather.

STOPPING THE FIRST YEAR.

Pinch off the leader when about two feet high, and stop all laterals at two joints. About the first of September withdraw water gradually, only giving sufficient to keep the vine from flagging; by so doing you will have well ripened roots and canes about the first of October. The pots may then be placed in a cool, dry cellar or shed, where they will be protected from frost and mice—first cutting the canes down to two inches This concludes the first year's treatment.

SECOND YEAR—GROWING CANES FOR EARLY FORCING.

Pot vines selected for early forcing, should be brought into a temperature of 40° to 45°, about the first of February. First soak the whole contents of the pot in good, moderately strong, clear manure water, setting the pot for two hours in a tub partly filled with such a solution—the drainage of a barn-yard or manure heap,—or prepared by stirring up some well rotted manure in water, and dipping off the clear liquid when it has settled. The decomposition of the manure is hastened, and the solution is improved by the addition of a small quantity of potash or wood ashes, say half a pound of potash or half a peck of ashes to one hundred pounds of manure.

Increase the temperature to the first of March, about 10°. Water sparingly, merely to keep the soil moist, till the vines break shoots two or three inches long, which will be about the first of April.

SHIFTING POTS.

Now shift the vines from seven to eleven inch pots, making slight but well secured drainage, and filling the pot with properly prepared soil. Good, turfy, half rotted sods, or good loam from an old pasture, with a handful or two of fine bone dust, or our special fertilizer, to each pot, and a little well decomposed stable manure, makes an excellent compost. Pot firmly, being careful not to bruise the roots in pressing down the soil, and place in the pot a strong stake three feet six inches long.

The temperature of the house may now be increased to 60° or 65° at night, and 10° or 15° more by day. Give air moderately at the top of the house, and keep the walls, floors, and whole house, in clear days, well sprinkled with water, so as to secure a very moist atmosphere.

STOPPING, TO MAKE DWARFS FOR EARLY FORCING.

By the middle of April, the vines will have made five or six inches growth, short-jointed and solid. Pinch off the leading shoot about one inch above the fourth eye. The three lower leaves will now develope very rapidly, and the lateral of the upper eye will make its appearance. When the upper lateral has grown two joints long, pinch it off within one inch of the main cane. The main eye will then start. If the three lower eyes are not very prominent, let the lateral of the upper eye run to three or four joints, in order to allow time for the lower eyes to develope their laterals. But when the lower eyes are very prominent, and the lower laterals are well developed, you may take off entirely the upper lateral.

The leader will start rapidly when the upper lateral is removed. As soon as the leader has made a few inches growth, pinch back the three lower laterals to one joint each. As soon as the leader has made five joints, pinch it off as before, and treat the new portion of the main cane as we directed for the first portion; that is, encouraging the growth or stopping the laterals as required by their condition and progress.

As soon as the wood begins to turn brown, near the roots, showing any indication of ripening, remove all the laterals to within one inch of the cane, up to the fourth eye. Now leave the cane to run rather freely, occasionally stopping both cane and laterals, at discretion, according to growth. If you allow the cane to grow too luxuriantly, you will be likely to lose the lower foliage before the wood is well ripened, which will be fatal to the fruiting of the lower eyes the following season; and an excess of cane, above sixteen eyes, will encumber the pot with an excessive quantity of roots.

By the middle of July, the last stopping will be performed. About the middle of August, water sparingly; only give so much moisture as will keep the vines from flagging. In the middle or latter part of September, the vines will show indications of going to rest, the foliage becoming yellow. About the first of October the pots may be placed in a cool cellar, where they will get moderate light; keep the soil just moist, admit cool air, but protect them from frost.

When the pots are placed in the cellar, cut down the

vines to two feet, or two feet six inches, still preserving the foliage as long as possible. The vines should be cut back a month before the foliage is gone, which gives the wood plenty of time to heal, so as to prevent bleeding when started in the spring.

SECOND YEAR CONTINUED—TREATMENT OF VINES FOR LATE CROPS.

We will now consider the second year's treatment of vines grown for ordinary purposes, say for fruiting from the first of July to the first of September.

Bring these pots out of the cellar about the first or middle of April, and place them in a tub of liquid manure for two hours, as directed for early forcing. Then put them into the green-house, or cold vinery. If the weather is severe, cover them at night with a few leaves, litter, cloth or canvas, to give them some protection from frost.

About the first of May the eyes will commence to break. Disbud down to the two lowest and strongest eyes.

SHIFTING POTS.

Now shift the vines to eleven inch pots, filling the vacant space with sod, compost and special fertilizers, as before directed for forcing. Select the strongest eye, giving preference to the lowest eye, and pot close up to the shoulder of this eye, so as to get new roots immediately from the new wood. Water very carefully, till the roots extend to the outside of the pot; apply the water only to the ball of earth from the old pot, and not to the whole soil. A little basin may be made, with a rim of soil or sod, so as to keep the water near the stem of the vine. If you water the whole contents of the pot, the new soil will become sour before the roots penetrate it. This is a point of the first importance.

STOPPING, AND MANAGEMENT.

The vine will now be stopped in precisely the same way, and treated in all respects as directed for vines intended for forcing.

The general management of the pot vine in the vinery will also be the same, in respect to ventilation, temperature, moisture, &c., as that of vines in the border.

Shorten the canes back to two feet, or two feet six inches, say about the first of November, still allowing the leaves to remain on till they fall off naturally, and the vines go to repose. About the first of December, place the pots in a cool cellar, to preserve them from frost; never allow the contents of the pots to become dust dry, but keep the soil always slightly moist.

TOP-DRESSING, COMPOSTS FOR FRUIT.

Before placing the pots in the cellar, remove all the old soil you can from the pots, without injury to the roots, and apply a top-dressing, to promote the formation of fruit. This will decompose, and gradually incorporate itself with the mass of the soil, and will answer nearly as well as if you remove the vine from the pot, and shift to a larger pot, with an increase of compost. The usual top-dressing is composed of rich loam, bone dust, cow dung, or well rotted stable manure, as before. But this dressing, although with the after application of liquid manure it will afford good grapes in abundance, does not meet the full requirements of the fruiting vine, and consequently cannot be expected to produce the largest, most perfectly colored, and highly flavored bunches.

The special manures required for *the fruiting vine*, are carbonaceous matter, silicate of potash, alkaline phosphates, tartrate of potash, and a small proportion of ammonia. The best method of supplying substances affording these ingredients, will be given in another part of this work.

THIRD YEAR—EARLY FORCING.

After the vines are cut back, at the end of the second season, say first of October, remove as much of the soil as possible, and top-dress as directed for the common vines. Keep them in a cool place for one month.

About the first of November remove the pots to a pit, and place them in a bottom heat of 75° to 80°, under a solar heat of 50° to 60°. Water sparingly till the buds break. In one month the eyes will begin to swell.

During the first month, the pots may be placed in the pit with *the canes bent down*, and the pit kept covered with mats quite dark, thus increasing the heat and humidity, which greatly promote the bursting of the eyes.

TEMPERATURE, MOISTURE, ETC.

In the beginning of the second month, when the buds are just bursting, the pots may be removed from the pit to the hot-house, and placed in a bottom heat of 80° to 90°, in an atmosphere of 65° by day and 60° at night, increasing 10° or 15° by sun heat. It is important to break the buds slowly.

After the buds are fully formed, and just as the leaves begin to show, maintain a dry atmosphere, for a few days, till the foliage is developed.

Let the vines go along at the above temperature till they begin to show fruit. After the foliage is developed, increase the moisture of the atmosphere.

After the fruit shows, keep the temperature of atmosphere at 60° to 65° at night, and 75° to 80° by day. Continue bottom heat as before.

Just as the vines come in flower, keep the atmosphere excessively moist; increase the heat for a few days, and *air freely.*

As soon as the fruit shows, stop the shoots upon which the bunches appear, at one or two joints beyond each bunch intended to be preserved. Usually two or three bunches show at the third, fourth and fifth joints. Select the best bunch on each shoot for preservation, giving the preference to the one nearest the main stem, and remove all the rest. Stop all laterals, leaving one new leaf every time, and continue to do so till the fruit commences to stone; then desist stopping altogether. By this method of stopping, the leaves of the laterals become almost as large as the main leaves, at least three times the size they usually attain under some of the old methods of summer pruning. One very large, well developed leaf is worth more to the vine than half a dozen small, imperfect leaves.

Thin the fruit as soon as you can see the berry formed. This is highly important. Leave about seven bunches on a vine two feet six inches high. Thin the berries or bunches of free setting grapes very thin, say leave only twenty per cent. of the berries; a bunch of four hundred berries, thin to sixty or eighty. You will get as much weight of fruit, far superior in size, color, and flavor, by so doing.

Continue to pinch-in the laterals closely, leaving one new leaf every time, as before directed, till the fruit commences to stone; then cease stopping and pinching and encourage the growth of foliage as much as possi ble. Should any of the laterals grow very strongly, stop them at any time, to keep the plant in proper form.

The temperature is to be continued for Hamburghs, and all kinds except Muscats, (which require 5° to 10° higher temperature,) at 65° to 70°, nights, and from 75° to 85°, days, admitting air freely. Watch for red spider closely, and if found, syringe heavily with clear, soft, tepid water; wash bricks with lime and sulphur, and place them on the hottest part of the pipes or flue.

Water freely with clear liquid manure, two or three times a week, (made with rain water only,) as warm, or warmer than the temperature of the house, using simple rain water also, as required.

Keep the top of the house slightly open night and day, for ventilation: and air very freely after the first symptoms of coloring, in favorable weather.

Grapes so grown in pots will ripen, about the middle of April, on a vine two feet six inches high, with ordinary culture, seven bunches, and with first-rate culture, eight to ten bunches.

When the fruit is quite ripe, the pots may be removed to any dry, warm room, set on a table in the dwelling, and the fruit will keep for two months on the vines.

FOR LATE FORCING,

Bring forward the pots into a bottom heat, at any time previous to the first of April, and pursue the same course as in early forcing.

COMMON MANAGEMENT OF POTS IN THE COLD VINERY, OR ORCHARD HOUSE.

Bring the pots out of the cellar about the middle of April, having top-dressed them the fall before, and soak them in manure water. Bend down the canes, as directed for vines in forcing, until the buds are well broken, say two inches long. Then stake them upright. Use very dilute manure water freely, or the special fertilizers required by the grape, increasing the strength of the manures as the vines gain vigor.

Treat the vines in all respects as before directed for forcing, and for common vineries, as to stopping, manuring, &c.

These pots will fruit with other vines in August and September.

The pots may also, if convenient, be brought along gradually in the hot-house, and fruited from time to time in the cold vinery, before the vines in the borders, so as to ripen at the end of June, or first of July. They may then be removed to a cool room, and if well ripened, and the bunches are properly thinned, they may be kept till the first of October upon the vines in excellent condition.

Late grapes in pots in the cold vinery, such as West's St. Peters and Muscats, Lady Down's Seedling, &c., will not ripen before the first of October. They may then be removed, about the middle of October, to some dry, airy, light room, and with abundance of air in dry weather, they may be kept in fine condition till Christmas, and with care, till the first of February or March.

Thus, by this process, with a little assistance in the hot-house, say two months in spring, you may have a succession of grapes in pots, from the first of August till the first of February, six months in the year; and by pot vine culture in the hot-house and cold vinery, you may have grapes every month in the year, if desired.

Grape Culture in Vineyards and Gardens.

The following directions are intended for small or large vineyards, or the garden culture of grapes on trellises, for table use and wine.

SOIL FOR THE GRAPE.

The best soil for a vineyard is undoubtedly a good sandy loam, resting upon a gravelly and but slightly clayey sub-soil. If the soil contain a good deal of soft, rotten rock, mica, and especially limestone, so much the better. Soft rock and mica, by their gradual decomposition, furnish potash, or silicate of potash, which, with lime, constitute two of the most important inorganic elements of the grape. A good supply of black, carbonaceous loam, is essential to the soil of a vineyard, and if not present, must be added by sod and peat composts, or plenty of well rotted manure and straw mulching. It is not necessary, under the method of culture recommended in this work, that the soil should be trenched three feet deep, or more, as is advised by some writers. Indeed, if the soil be good, and the sub-soil be porous or well drained, we think deep trenching not only unnecessary but positively injurious to the long-continued health and fruitfulness of the vine. If the vineyard be deeply plowed and sub-soiled, or otherwise worked, so as to give eighteen inches of good mellow, well pulverized earth, it is all that is required. We do not desire to invite the roots of the grape down into the sub-soil. We do not consider it necessary to manure the whole soil heavily before planting a vineyard. It is a waste of valuable material. We prefer to work the manure into the surface of the earth, from year to year, as needed, and thus invite the roots *upwards* into the warm, rich surface soil, instead of downwards into the cold sterile sub-soil.

We do not consider a very rich garden soil by any means the best for the grape. It will cause too luxuriant a growth of wood. We prefer to apply a top dressing of good well-rotted stable manure, hog manure, or slaughter-house offal, well composted with peat or sod, as a top dressing, in the fall or early spring, before using the special manures recommended in another part of this work. This will enable the vines to perfect a good crop of fruit, or to form the necessary amount of wood, each year, without exciting a late growth of succulent canes, liable to be winter-killed. As to the quantity of stimulating manure required, we will say that it should be about the same as for an acre of wheat, say twenty to fifty horse-loads of good, rich, carbonaceous and ammoniacal compost per acre, every year or two; or 300 to 600 pounds of good guano, composted in the same way, or mixed with an equal bulk of plaster, well moistened, a week or two before using it.

The special manures required for a crop of grapes, in the vineyard and in pot culture, will be described in another section of this work.

PREPARATION OF THE SOIL FOR GRAPE VINES.

The thorough preparation of the soil for the grape border, or the vineyard, by ploughing, harrowing, rolling, spading, raking, &c., is probably of more consequence than even that of manuring; and by "thorough preparation" we mean more than the reader, unless he is a skilful cultivator, has any idea of. We mean *twelve* ploughings and harrowings, instead of two. We mean one fall ploughing, left rough for winter freezing. We mean the breaking up of all lumps of earth with the spade; the most perfect and minute division of the soil that is possible, so that it shall be left at last, as light as bolted flour. It is in such a soil as this that the grape vine delights, a soil which has been worked over and over, in a partially dry state, a dozen times at least, and allowed to sink into a beautiful consistency by its own gravity, without any pressing or treading. We are quite of the opinion, that a good old pasture soil, where no trees, grain, or vines have grown for twenty years, is the best of all soils for the grape, and that it cannot be greatly improved, for the growth of the vine, for a year or two, by any sort of manuring whatever. In such a soil, the vine grows naturally, luxuriantly, and healthfully. It is the best of all soils for a grape border, and only when we come to fruit the vine heavily do we need manures and fertilizers to sustain it. It is a great mistake to suppose that a grape vine, newly set in a border, must at once be fed with an abundance of rich and stimulating manure. There is no objection to the application of an abundance of well decomposed sod or peat compost, made with one-fourth part of stable manure, and some leaf mould and bone dust. But people do not rightly understand the meaning of the phrase "well decomposed." It requires either the use of powerful chemical agents, or a year or two of time to render stable manure and peat really "well decomposed." It must be reduced to a state analogous to that of an old garden soil, in which it is impossible to distinguish any of the various ingredients of which it is composed. In this condition, all the vegetable matter is converted into a sort of humus, and all inorganic substances are either in a soluble state or ready to become so; the acids and alkalies are in a neutral state, or in the shape of harmless salts; moisture is abundant, and ammonia is not wanting. Such preparation of the soil, and such composts, suit the grape vine a great deal better than animal offal and raw bones, which in vine borders we trust have had their day.

PLANTING, PRUNING AND TRAINING.

Take good, strong, two-year old plants, set in rows six or eight feet apart, and two feet apart in the rows. Set in a slanting direction, about four inches under the surface of the earth, close up to the young wood of the last year's growth, or bury two inches of the young wood, and cut down to two eyes.

When the vine breaks, select the strongest of the two eyes, giving the preference to the one nearest the ground, and remove the other bud, leading up only one cane. Tie perpendicularly on the trellis, and pinch in when it reaches the top wire or bar, say four or five feet from the surface of the ground. The laterals will now begin to grow. Stop all laterals back to one joint, and continue to stop in the same way till the middle of August, leaving one new leaf on each joint every time. If the vine grows very luxuriantly, the laterals may be allowed to extend to two or three joints, to prevent the main buds from bursting, as it is well known that if the main buds be destroyed, the fruit which would otherwise be produced next season, will be lost. After the middle of August, the vine may be allowed to grow without further care or stopping.

As soon as the leaves fall, cut back every other cane within two or three eyes of the ground. Prune the canes intended to be fruited the next year to the top of the trellis, and cut back all laterals to one inch of the main stem.

For trellises, in small vineyards, we recommend posts of good size, set about ten or twelve feet apart, with wires run lengthwise the rows, say about six to eight inches apart. Number twelve wire is about the right size for economy; larger wire would no doubt be better, where the first cost is not much regarded.

When cold weather sets in, it is highly useful, even for hardy vines, to lay them down, as you would raspberry vines, and cover them with soil. The labor is not great, in gardens and small vineyards, and the benefit derived from such winter protection well repays the trouble or expense. If the winter is very severe, the canes will escape injury, and even if mild, they will come out much better for this protection. Mulch with next year's compost.

FRUITING THE VINES.

In the spring, as soon as the peach trees are in bloom, uncover the fruiting canes, and sling them carelessly for a time, not perpendicularly, but horizontally on the lowest wire, thus bending them down till the shoots have made a growth of two inches. Then tie them up perpendicularly, with pieces of Cuba matting. As soon as the fruit buds begin to break, there being generally two together, remove the weaker one, which is usually the under or lower one, select the bunch nearest the main stem for preservation, and stop two joints from the bunch. Then stop all laterals, leaving one new leaf every time, till the fruit takes its second swelling after forming stones (during the stoning process, the berries swell but little, say for four or five weeks,) then allow the foliage to grow without further check.

By this process the leaves will grow very large, the fruit will be well shaded, and a good crop of large bunches of well colored and well ripened fruit will ordinarily be produced.

During the stoning of the fruit, if convenient, water the vines liberally, and apply liquid manure, or during a shower, special grape fertilizers. Afterwards keep the grape borders dry.

After the crop of fruit is gathered, and the leaves have fallen, the fruiting canes will be cut down, leaving two eyes on the new wood.

The vine should be allowed to bear only a specimen of fruit the second year after planting. The third year a fair crop may be taken, say one bunch on each shoot. When the vine is fully established, say the fourth or fifth year, about six pounds of fruit may be taken from four feet of cane, or twelve bunches. More bunches may be obtained from this length of cane, but the fruit will not be so fine.

After some years, by this process, the stem of the old cane will become too long to be fruited with advantage, and the roots will have penetrated too deeply into the soil to be further worked with success. The top of the vine may then be layered, and a fresh plant, of a vigorous character will be speedily produced, to take the place of the old vine, having its roots, where all vine roots should be, near the surface of the earth.

THE GROWING VINES.

When the vines intended to be grown for the next season's fruit break strong in the spring, pinch back the laterals to two or three joints, so as not to burst the main eyes, leaving one new leaf as before directed, every time, and stop the tip of the vine at the top of the trellis. Continue the same process of stopping till the middle of August, when the vine may be allowed to grow without further check.

In autumn, cut back the cane to within two or three inches of the top wire or bar of the trellis, and lay down for winter protection, as before.

Vines may be grown in this way tied to stakes, or upon arbors, and may be allowed to extend to a height of six to fifteen feet if desired, so as to cover an arbor with foliage, with nearly as good results as upon low trellises in the vineyard, though the crop of fruit will not be so fine or so valuable as upon low trellises.

SPECIAL FEATURES OF THIS SYSTEM.

It will be perceived that we place the vines only two feet apart, thus growing more than double the usual number of plants upon a given line of border or trellis. By this means we are able to cut down one-half the vines every year, and still have more fruiting canes than by any other plan. The number of roots is greatly increased, and hence the wood is fully nourished and sustained. Observe, it is not wood alone that produces fruit, but roots. By our system we double and treble the number of grape roots in a border, and hence have a vastly increased source of supply for our fruit. The ordinary system, we are quite convinced, taxes the roots too severely, and hence you have too frequently, a large quantity of poor, immature fruit. Under this system, we have plenty of roots, and an increased number of vines, and manage so as to let them do all they are able, and no more. We concentrate, as before observed, the whole strength of the vine upon a small quantity of fruit, near the ground, giving to each vine all it can perfect, and the result is larger bunches and finer fruit, of higher flavor, and a larger and surer crop on the same space of ground.

The *rest* from fruiting which the vines obtain, under this system, every other year, does much to keep them in a healthy state, and does not exhaust their resources for forming fruit so rapidly. It is a sort of fallow, giving time for the collection and elaboration of the elements of fruit, for the ensuing season, which may almost be supposed to be drawn from the earth and the atmosphere, during this season of rest, and stored up in the cells and tissues of the vine, for future use. Or, if this be too fanciful an idea, unsustained by vegetable physiology, or practical science, still we may say that the soil, during this period of rest, has time to decompose, and to devclope the elements of fruit, and to collect such elements from the atmosphere, from manure and from rains; and is better prepared to present these materials in a soluble form to the roots of the vine, when demanded by the next crop of fruit.

But whatever may be the theory or the philosophy of the facts, we know that the vine, when cultivated upon this system, will yield larger and finer crops of grapes, upon the same extent of ground, than upon any other that we have ever seen practised, and the fruit ripens much earlier, which last is a point of no little importance.

It will be observed, that a vine may be grown, upon this system, fifteen feet in length, upon arbors, or in the vinery, if desired; but for vineyard culture, or in small gardens, we advise trellises only four to six feet high, on account partly of the greater case with which such trellises may be erected and tended, though we are quite convinced that four to six feet of vine is enough for the roots, under ordinary culture, and that a better crop will be produced upon that length of wood than upon longer canes. Under higher culture, and with extra care, in the cold grapery, longer canes of the foreign grapes may be employed, as will be noticed in the proper place. So, also, on arbors, where shade is more of an object than fruit, the canes may be allowed to run ten or fifteen feet to the top of the trellis or arbor. But where you wish for a good crop of choice, well-colored, and well-ripened fruit, low trellises and short canes, (say three to five feet high,) grown upon this single stem renewal system, will give the best results.

It is so rare a thing to see first rate Isabella grapes, that few persons know to what perfection this grape may be brought by high culture and proper concentration. Much may be done to perfect this grape, by the system of management which we have described, but still more by the judicious and scientific application of special fertilizers, as will be described in the chapter on Soils and Manures. As the pea may be made more melting, and the potato more mealy by the use of lime, and the strawberry more delicious by the use of tan, so the grape may be rendered more luscious, vinous, and sugary, by the application of proper fertilizers, as well as larger and more beautiful to the eye.

PLANTING CUTTINGS, STAKES, ETC.

Large or small vineyards, or borders for arbors, may of course be planted with cuttings, or with transplanted cuttings started in a nursery, or with plants struck from single eyes in pots, and trained to stakes instead of trellises.

It is unnecessrry for us to describe all these processes in detail, as we presume no one will undertake grape culture without being familiar with these elementary matters; or if they desire such information, may easily find it in any general work on the grape.

We will only say that in planting cuttings, we prefer slips of only two joints or eyes, instead of cuttings four or five joints long. We set the short cutting with only one bud below the surface of the ground, which makes a plant with a short root, whereas a cutting four or five joints long, plunged a foot or more deep into the soil, forms its "foot roots," as they are styled, too far below the best part of the soil, and never will form so good a vine as if cut shorter, and rooted entirely within four inches of the surface. Our reasons for shallow planting will be given in full in another part of this work.

MULCHING VINEYARDS.

Under the system of shallow planting recommended in this work, it is indispensable that the soil of vineyards and grape borders should be constantly mulched, especially in summer; and indeed under any system of planting in any part of the United States where the Catawba will ripen, it will be found highly useful to shade the ground in some way from the direct rays of the sun, in July and August. Any kind of litter will, of course, answer this purpose; charcoal, or tan composted with lime, would be very good; but the best mulch, beyond all question, would be the leaves of trees.

To mulch an acre of vineyard with any of these substances effectually, would cost almost as much as to manure it with the best of fertilizers; and hence we can scarcely expect it will be done unless some cheap means of accomplishing this object can be suggested.

One very cheap and efficient means of mulching a vineyard, which we have practised to some extent and find quite satisfactory, is to plant in a drill between the rows of vines, the Southern Field Pea or Cow Pea, a leguminous plant very much employed in Virginia and other Southern States, as a green crop to renovate worn-out soils, by ploughing under while in flower. This plant will grow in any soil, if supplied with lime, and will endure the severest drouth without flagging. It sends its roots very deeply into the sub-soil, and obtains the larger portion of its nutriment from the atmosphere. It has a stalk almost as large and firm as that of a tomato vine, and spreads widely over the surface of the ground. In ninety days it produces as much mulching material, and as much green matter of tops and roots, for manure, as an acre of good clover, and of precisely the same character and value, either for manure or food. It is well known, we presume, to all intelligent readers of modern agricultural literature, that the stalk and vine of the pea is richer in nitrogen, (or ammoniacal substances,) and alkaline salts, than the best of wheat or rye straw, and hence must form a very valuable material for mulching or manure.

Our method of planting the pea is this: we cultivate the spaces between the rows of vines very lightly with the horse-hoe, in the spring, and about the first of June open a very shallow furrow with a small plow, in each space, and drop the peas in this furrow or drill, so as to form hills about two or three feet apart in the drill, say ten or fifteen peas in a hill, and cover with the plow or hoe. Afterwards cultivate a little to keep down weeds, just as you would ordinary peas or corn. It takes about half a bushel, or less, of seed to plant an acre of vineyard in this way, and the seed costs about $1.25 per bushel in Baltimore.

This pea vine makes a very perfect shade for the roots of the grape, while growing, during July and August, and when cut down, just as it comes into flower, in the early part of September, furnishes a large quantity of valuable litter for mulching and manure. It does not exhaust the soil, because it returns to it more of carbon and nitrogen than it abstracts from it; and it only takes potash, lime, &c., from the sub-soil, to return it to the top-soil in a state better fitted for the food of plants. We have used the kind of pea known as the *clay*, or cow pea, and also the *black eye* pea. The *early black* is said to be the best for a northern climate.

We consider this method of mulching vineyards very economical, and amply sufficient to protect the roots of vines from excessive heat and drouth. Since we commenced this practice, we have learned that a similar method of mulching has been employed in France for many years. In Redding's Treatise on Modern Wines, published in London, in 1833, he states that, "in some parts of France, *lupines* (a kind of pea) are sown among the vines, and buried when in flower around their roots, where they decay; a practice found to be of *singular utility to the crops.*" Again, he says, of vineyards in the island of Madeira, " some growers use animal manures, which others reject, and as the French do, they sow *lupines* among the vines, and bury them at their roots."

In some of the letters written by Mr. Longworth, of Cincinnati, on the rot in grapes, he states that in several instances, vineyards which were planted on dry, porous soil, and accidentally *mulched with weeds*, escaped the rot, while vineyards in the immediate vicinity, which were kept clean, and not mulched, suffered severely. These passages will be found in Mr. Buchanan's work on the grape.

We believe that only by shallow planting and good mulching, can we maintain the continued healthfulness of vineyards, while by trenching, heavy manuring, and deep planting, we shall be sure, sooner or later, to induce rot and mildew, and the final destruction of the vines.

Vines in City Yards.

VINES on trellises in city yards and small village gardens, may be most conveniently and profitably managed upon the single stem renewal system of training herein recommended. The borders for such vines in the city should, if possible, be formed of brick-work, detached from the adjacent cold, compact and useless soil of the yard, and underdrained by tiles conducted into a cess-pool or culvert, in order to render them warmer and dryer, spring and fall; and a mulching of litter in summer will greatly assist in retaining moisture. Twice the number of vines will of course be grown as under the ordinary system, and only half of them fruited each year. Vines so managed will make an astonishing growth in a single season, often running to the height of the tallest trellis, if well supplied with appropriate fertilizers; while the foliage of the fruiting and the growing canes will afford quite as much shade as vines grown with long branches in the ordinary way, and they can be much more easily and systematically trained, and produce more and better fruit. Vines on city trellises, allowed to ramble at will for the sake of shade, and sparingly fed with proper nutriment, seldom fruit for many years, and even when they do bear, the fruit is of little value. But when grown upon our system, with a good exposure, they will not only make ample shade, and present a pleasing object to the eye, but they can be made to produce large crops of the most delicious grapes every year.

For the method of training adapted to city trellises, see the section upon the common vineyard. The only variation that should be made in training for the high trellis, is this: the vine should not be stopped at the height of four or five feet, but should be allowed to run to the full height of the trellis, and if the wood to the full height should not happen to be strong and solid, the first season, it should be cut back to the strong wood before fruiting the first time. After the vine gets older, it will make strong wood to the full height of the tallest trellis, in one season, provided it be well fed with proper fertilizers. We think this system of training for city trellises, will be much admired when once it has been tried.

VINES ON ARBORS.

Vines on arbors, in villa and cottage lots, and small gardens, may be trained upon our system with great satisfaction and advantage. Plant the vines two feet or less apart, and train with a single stem, as in the vineyard, and fruit every other cane each year. If the border be good, and well fertilized, the vines will run to the top of the arbor in a single season, and afford immediate shade and abundance of fruit, far surpassing, in respect to beauty and profit, vines grown in the common way.

Vines on old arbors may be renewed by layers from the old stock, and trained upon this system with great ease and success, entirely renovating the old vines, and changing the system of culture in one year, to the great delight of the owner.

A very pretty arbor may be made upon the south side of a barn or house, by planting posts two feet high, say four or five feet from the wall or barn, and running rafters from these posts to the barn or house, just like the rafters of a vinery. Strain wires lengthwise of this arbor, plant and train the vines on the inside of the rafters, and you have a sort of out of door vinery, (minus the glass,) a very novel and interesting object, and a very admirable method of growing grapes. The bunches of grapes, when vines are trained on this plan, will hang under the foliage, affording a degree of shade which is very useful to them, and a current of cool, moist air will constantly pass through the arbor, which is highly beneficial to the vines. For the Catawba grape especially, this would be an excellent method; and if the borders were slightly elevated, and well drained, so as to be easily dried off in the fall, a sure crop of fine, well ripened grapes might be obtained, every year, from such an arbor, at least as far north as Philadelphia. Farther north, it might be advisable to provide some protection against frost, such as an awning, which could be easily contrived for such a lean-to arbor. And here we may observe that it will be found of great advantage, especially in working upon our system, always to bury your canes intended for fruit the next year, in winter, and to mulch well in very cold weather.

Arbors may also be made with roofs pitching both ways, like a spar-roofed vinery, instead of oval, with great economy and advantage, upon which vines will grow and fruit upon the one stem renewal system with great success.

Vines may also be grown, upon this system, tied to small stakes, say five or six feet high, set anywhere in a small lawn or garden, just as you would set out a dwarf cherry or currant bush, and much fruit may be obtained, of excellent quality, while the vines will form very pleasing objects in your grounds. Of course, two vines should be planted to each stake, one for fruiting, and one for growing wood; and if you please, you may train them upon small pieces of wood nailed across the stakes, or far prettier, upon the stump of a tree, or upon any sort of upright fancy trellises that your inventive faculty may suggest. This is a method of planting and training well adapted to any small piece of vacant ground in any yard or garden, where formal arbors or trellises would be inadmissible; and is quite as good a plan for obtaining fruit as any other, and more novel and interesting.

Renewing an Old Vine, or Arbor of Vines.

MANY persons have old vines, which, from being badly pruned and trained, fail to give either good or abundant fruit, and yet the owners are loth to dig them up, because they afford much shade, and they are fearful that they may not succeed in producing other vines more systematic in form, or more productive. Such persons often ask us if they can bring their old vines into our system of pruning, with any success. We answer, yes. Our method of doing it is this: we prepare a new border alongside of the old vine, and layer all the wood that can be made available, burying the body of the cane some six inches deep, along the border, and bringing up the branches and young wood as layers, at points where we desire to locate the new vines. The whole vine may be coiled up like a spiral spring, and buried at one spot, and a layer or layers may then be brought up, within a small space of ground, from the young wood; or the branches may be carried any distance under ground, and brought up wherever desired. The roots of the old vine should at the same time be abundantly supplied with appropriate fertilizers, to promote the rapid formation of wood; and the growth which may be obtained in a single season, by this plan, is often truly surprising.

Other methods of obtaining layers, without burying the whole cane, will readily occur to persons acquainted with the nature of the vine, and it is therefore unnecessary to describe them.

As soon as the new layers are well rooted, say at the beginning of the second season, they may be separated from the old vine, and thus a great number of young and vigorous plants may be obtained, in place of one old, barren, and almost worthless cane. We have renewed several old vines and arbors in this way, producing twenty or thirty new, healthy, fruitful canes, ten and fifteen feet in length, in a single season, where before existed only an old, tangled mass of barren wood, unsightly and useless, even for purposes of shade, to the great delight and astonishment of the owner. Our system of pruning gives as much shade on arbors as any other, and vastly more fruit, of an infinitely superior quality. If shade high up on the trellis or arbor be an object, the vine need not be cut back so low as for the vineyard, but its fruiting wood may be taken from any height that may be desired.

Ohio German System of Grape Culture.

GROWING FRUIT AND WOOD ON THE SAME STEM.—BOWING VINES.

The "Ohio German System" of Grape Culture as it has been called, which is practised in the vineyards near Cincinnati, consists in growing one or more fruiting shoots, or bows, and one or more new shoots for the next season's fruiting bows, in a single year, on the same stem.

Now it is a sort of law of nature that you cannot successfully grow wood and fruit at the same time; or at least it is true that the stimulating manures which best promote a growth of wood or vine, are not favorable to fruit, and those manures which best promote the formation of fruit, do not excite an active growth of wood. A heavy crop of fruit always checks the growth of a tree or vine, and in many fruit trees renders them sterile the next year. Hence, we argue that it is not wise to attempt to grow a heavy crop of fruit, and the next year's wood on the same vine, or from the same grape root.

Under our system, we concentrate the whole force of

the grape root, for one year, upon the fruit, and aid this if you please, by special manure directed to that object. The next year we cut down the entire vine, and give it time to rest and form new wood, stimulating it, if need be, by proper means, to accomplish that object. This we think is far the best method.

The *bowing* of vines we consider quite unnecessary. We agree with Dr. C. W. GRANT, the eminent grape grower of Iona, New York, who says that "the disposition of the vine is strongly upward, and under ordinary circumstances will not continue to make bearing-wood, for a succession of seasons, through a greater perpendicular height than four feet, and even within these limits the upper portions will show the greatest vigor of growth, and the lower the best flavor, but not the largest or the most beautiful bunches."

The *bowing* plan is adopted at Cincinnati to prevent the too free growth of the top of the vine, and to equalize the flow of sap to all parts of the cane.

We accomplish the same object, as will be seen by reference to our directions for the management of vines in the vineyard and in pot culture, by slinging the vines in the spring, in a horizontal or bowing form, for a short time, till the lower buds break and form shoots two or three inches long, when the vines may be raised up and trained perpendicularly without any injurious effect upon the lower shoots. Once the lower eyes get a good start they will obtain sufficient sap to form good fruit, and the natural tendency to excessive growth in the top will be so effectually checked as to render continued bowing quite unnecessary.

In the vinery or hot-house, all first class gardeners bend down the canes in spring till the lower eyes break strongly, before ticing up the vines to the trellis, in order to ensure an equal diffusion of sap to all parts of the cane. This is all the bowing that is really necessary.

Our objection to the bowing plan is, that the vine cannot be so easily and effectually secured to the stake or trellis, and is more liable to be blown about by the wind, to the injury of the fruit, while it has a rough, straggling appearance, and does not form so pleasing an object to the spectator, as when trained in an erect position.

The Cold Vinery.

For the cold vinery, as well as the hot-house, we recommend, as of the first importance, small, shallow, detached borders, (which we will immediately proceed to describe) altogether inside of the house. The common border may, however, be used if preferred.

The inside border, at first, if true economy be consulted, should be made only two feet deep and three feet wide, resting upon a concrete bottom with six inches of small, rough stones, or oyster-shell drainage above it. Between the outer edge of the border and the front wall of the vinery, there should be a space of say four inches, formed by four inch brick work, to assist in keeping the frost out of the border. This space is kept open at the top to admit warm air from the house, and connected below with pipes, or tiles, or conductors constructed of brick, running through the drainage, to conduct the warm air under the border. This open space in front of the border, and the conductors of tiles or bricks, serve not only the purpose of keeping frost out of the border, but also, at all seasons to equalize the temperature of the border and the house, which is of great importance in vine culture. These air conductors are to be laid in the drainage, above the concrete, and may be formed by dry brickwork, making a tube four inches in diameter, or by four inch tiles, connecting with the open space between the border and the front wall, and opening into the house on the inner edge of the border, there passing through a wall of dry brick or stone, or even boards, merely to keep the inside edge of the border in place.

The border, when constructed on this plan, will be entirely detached from the soil, both inside and outside of the house. It will rest upon drainage, laid upon solid, impervious concrete, and will have a wall, detached from the house, on the front and back. It will be situated like the earth in a pot or orchard-house tub, and will be, in fact, one immense pot or box, perfectly confining the roots of the vines within its own limits.

We feel entirely satisfied that this is the best method now known of constructing a vine border. The shallow border, entirely inside of the house, is now beginning to be employed by some of the best grape growers in Europe and America. The atmospheric conductors, though not entirely original with the writer, have been more largely employed and advocated by us than by any other writer or practical grape grower within our knowledge.

ATMOSPHERIC CONDUCTORS.

The philosophy of *Atmospheric Conductors*, under vine borders, we have presented in various articles published in the horticultural journals. The following is from an article on this subject, which we contributed to the Philadelphia Gardener's Monthly, for January, 1859 :—

"One of the chief points in the management of vineries, as all intelligent gardeners are aware, is to control and regulate the temperature of the borders, so as to give the roots an early start in the spring, and to put them into a state of repose early in the fall. If the growth of roots be too luxuriant in the fall, in consequence of excessive heat in the border, immature roots and wood will be the result, greatly to the detriment of the vine the ensuing season. So if the vine, by frost, prematurely lose its foliage, then the main roots cannot be matured, and a good 'break' of buds cannot be expected in the spring. There must be a perfect unity of action between the upper extremity of the vine and its roots, to ensure the highest degree of success in grape culture.

"In the fall, as we all know, the temperature of the atmosphere will often fall to 40° Fahrenheit, while the earth two feet under the surface is at 65°. On or about the 15th of November, 1857, the thermometer fell to 17°, and the foliage of many vines in cold houses was suddenly cut off, while the bottom heat of the borders was at 60°. Immature roots, which could not be expected to keep, were produced. Such vines must, of course, 'break' weakly in the spring; their great feeders are mainly destroyed, and they must create them again in the spring before they can make strong growth.

"In April the solar heat is often 75°, while the temperature of the earth is little higher than the freezing point. In such cases, the canes are, of course, unduly excited into action, while the roots are comparatively dormant, and the natural balance of the vine or the nice unity of action between the root and the wood, which it is so important to preserve, is destroyed.

"To attain the most perfect success in vine culture, it would be desirable to keep the border heat, in spring, about ten degrees above the solar heat, and to reduce the temperature of the border in autumn in the same proportion. As soon as the grape crop is matured, we should hasten, by all proper means, the ripening of roots and wood,—the border should be dried and cooled, and the roots thrown into a state of repose. As soon as the roots cease their functional action, the upper wood will be in a state of rest. So, in the spring, a quick heat in the border will start the roots at the same time with the canes, and a healthy growth of roots and wood must be the result of such harmonious action."

INSIDE BORDERS,

Are far preferable to borders extending partly beyond the front wall outside. Inside the house, in detached borders, we have the most perfect control of the vine, as to moisture, protection from frost, and the extent to which the roots may be permitted to extend downward. The expense of construction is much less, and the labor of covering and protecting them is saved. Large, deep borders are no longer advocated by the best grape growers, and hence there is no necessity for extending them beyond the limits of the house. All the plans which we shall present, for the culture of the vine in graperies, form part of one entire system of improved construction and management, which, it is believed, renders growing of grapes under glass much more economical and successful than by the old methods.

Before concreting the bottom of the border, remove the soil to the depth required, and level the border so as to descend about nine inches each way to the centre line, forming it so as to open into a drain built of bricks and mortar along the centre of the house, six inches square, falling below the concrete, but constructed so as to unite closely with it. That is to say, the drainage of the border, passing down the surface of the concrete, will fall into a drain built of bricks and mortar, running along the centre line, and falling six inches below it. The drain will of course have a proper fall from one end of the house to the other, and will discharge its contents, if any, by a waste pipe carried outside the house.

Before laying the concrete, well ram the bottom of the border, smooth and solid, and construct the middle drain.

CONCRETE.

We presume almost every body engaged in rural affairs, knows how to make concrete, but all may not know how to make it easily and perfectly. Our plan is this. We first construct a mortar-bed, of sufficient size, of boards. Then we slack one or more barrows of lime, as required, in a lime box or tub, and add water till it is reduced to the condition of thick cream or ordinary whitewash. Now draw or dip off the lime water, free from unslacked lumps or stone, and pour it into the mortar-bed, first having placed around its edges a layer of sand to keep the lime water from running off. Then shovel or wheel into the bed a quantity of course sand, gravel, and small, rough stones, sufficient to soak up nearly all the lime water. Commence at the outer edge of the heap, and hoe down and mix the mass, with a mason's hoe, working it up a little into good, coarse mortar, and tempering it with more lime water if needed, and as it is hoed down, shovel it over into a heap on the outer edge of the bed. Now it is ready for use. Let a laborer shovel this coarse mortar into a barrow, and deposit it upon the bottom of the border in a layer about two or three inches thick, smoothing it off with a hoe, trowel, or any other convenient instrument. If made with good, fresh lime and sand, gravel and stones, free from loam, and pretty rich with lime, it will set in twenty-four hours, and in a few days become very hard, and finally quite impervious to water or the roots of plants. If the lime be slacked in the mortar-bed, and not screened clear of lumps, the concrete will be much less perfect; and if the workmen attempt to wet the heap of sand and stones, by pouring lime water upon it, or to dig the heap when wet from the top, much time and labor will be expended in a useless manner.

DRAINAGE.

After the concrete has become solid, lay the atmospheric conductors across the border, and deposit the drainage material between and upon them, about six inches deep.

DIVIDED BORDERS.

In addition to placing the grape border altogether inside the house, and detaching it from the front wall and from the soil, we have also lately divided the border into sections two feet wide, by brick partitions, keeping every vine by itself, just as if the border consisted of a number of large pots or tubs. This method we like very much, and earnestly recommend it to the attention of grape growers. Each section of the border, intended for a single vine, will be three feet long, two feet wide, and two feet deep. The quantity of compost which this space will contain is amply sufficient to sustain a vine for several years, and when any danger of exhaustion is apprehended, it may easily be enlarged.

The advantages of divided borders are numerous and important. In the first place, there is no possibility, under such circumstances, that the stronger growing vines can interfere with or injure the weaker ones. At the same time, the weaker ones can be watered or manured freely, if desired, without affecting the vines on either side of them. Or, the strong growing kinds may be checked, if necessary, to make them fruitful, by giving less nutriment and less water. In the common border, extending outside of the house, it is almost impossible to induce the Muscats to ripen their wood, especially the king of all the Muscats, the Cannon Hall; while in pots, where we have full control of the moisture of the soil, we find no such difficulty, and the wood matures in the most perfect manner. Again, if you have any very weak or imperfect vines in your border, or some whose quality you do not like, you can take any one or more of them out, and replace them with more thrifty or more desirable kinds, without in the least disturbing the roots of other vines. In the common border it is almost impossible to remove a large, old vine, without doing great injury to the adjacent vines, nor can you grow a young vine, with good success, in a border full of the roots of older vines. Grafting or inarching may be resorted to in the case of the common border, but these operations it is sometimes difficult for amateurs to perform with success. Each vine, in the divided border, gets its allotted share of nutriment with the utmost certainty, and thus it is very easy to measure off the food for each carefully, or to try experiments with different fertilizing agents, or single ones, without the danger of affecting your whole house in case of error. But the ease with which you may change the vines in your house, already alluded to, is one of the most pleasing advantages. Vines may be grown in pots, of good size, ready for fruiting, and set in one of your large divisions in the border, either with or without its ball of earth, and it is only like shifting to a larger pot. It will be ready to fruit at once. At the time of making such changes of vines, you may also, if you choose, change the entire soil in each section of the border from which old vines are removed, without in the least disturbing other parts of the border. The fact is, that the arbitrary old system of making a large border, inside and outside of the house, and planting once for all, with no convenient way of changing your vines, and waiting years to fill the borders with roots and the house with wood, before you enjoy the fruits of your investment and labor, is really very absurd. In the small divided border, with well grown pot vines, you may fruit half your house, if you choose, the first year; and you may change your stock of varieties as often as you please, losing very little time or fruit by the operation. If you have any fears that the divisions of the border will be too small to sustain the vines, just reflect that a vine in a pot eleven inches in diameter, containing little more than half a cubic foot of soil, is capable of producing from five to ten pounds of well perfected grapes, and that the divisions of the border here described will contain twelve cubic feet of soil, and may easily be increased in size if desired, and the vines will be expected to bear only about twenty to thirty pounds of grapes once in two years. Borders have almost always been made too large, some of them contain five hundred cubic feet of soil to each vine, and immensely rich at that. Such borders really do more harm than good. In a few years they invariably become sodden and sour, and in many instances the grapes mildew and shank, or the vines die out altogether. The cost of such borders is very great, and altogether unnecessary. If you wish to improve a divided border without enlarging it, you can easily remove some of the top soil, and replace it with fresh, light, sweet, rich compost, or apply an increased quantity of special fertilizers. Or, we have no doubt that the vine might be lifted from a section of a divided border, late in the fall, its roots freed of old soil, or even washed out in warm water, and replanted in fresh soil, without material injury, if not with great advantage. Indeed we think that small detached and divided borders, entirely inside the house, will be found cheaper, more convenient and efficient than any other form of border, and will soon be universally adopted.

ROOFS OF VINERIES.

In this work we do not intend to consider at any length, the best methods of constructing hot-houses, or cold graperies, but we will suggest to amateurs in building new vineries, to be sure and have fixed roofs, with permanent bars, and uniform ventilation on the top, and not sliding sash, after the old method.

COMPOSTS AND SOIL FOR BORDERS.

Make the compost, for the vine border, of good loam from the surface of a well cultivated field, (not from an old garden,) where no trees have grown for many years, and where the soil is nearly in a virgin state, but not likely to be sour from excess of moist vegetable matter, or exhausted by heavy and injudicious cropping. Let this loam be mixed with one-third its bulk of sod from an old headland or pasture, finely chopped with a sharp spade or grubbing hoe. Add to about twenty one-horse loads of this mixture, about four bushels of good water-slacked lime, or better still, three bushels of lime and salt mixture, made by slacking three bushels of lime with one bushel of salt dissolved in water, and frequently turned over for two weeks before use. If you have any wood ashes, add four bushels of unleached, or ten bushels of leached ashes. Turn over this heap twice, moistening it well with water, if not wet by rain, and waiting till it becomes pretty dry before turning. Be very careful and not turn the heap when in the least degree wet. The dryer the better, for turning and chopping. In fact this compost should be made under a shed, or covered with boards, if exposed to too much rain. Now add to this compost of about twenty horse-loads, say five one-horse loads of well-rotted stable manure, horse and cow dung, or its equivalent of any rich nitrogenous compost; and ten horse loads of soft, rotten rock of a limestone or micaceous character, and sand; or rotten rock and sandy road-scrapings from a turnpike. If you choose to add ten to twenty bushels of finely crushed bones, or one or two barrels of good super-phosphate of lime, or our special fertilizer, it will be useful, although the bones will serve little other use than as a substitute for sand, and the super-phosphate of lime or fertilizer may be better applied upon the surface of the border when needed. Let your vines, at first, rest in good natural soil, well manured, and they will form plenty of vigorous wood; afterwards apply special fertilizers, as needed, to produce and perfect the fruit, and the highest success will be attained.

Put no carcasses of animals, offal of slaughter-houses, night soil, guano, or any rich animal matter, or other stimulating manure into or under the border, beyond what we have advised; although if the stable manure be poor, it may be made a little richer by the addition of a bag of guano, without injury. Let the compost, made up as directed, be kept moderately moist, and turned frequently, chopped and pulverized as much as possible, so as to reduce it to a state of minute division. The finer the particles of the soil the better. Again we say, turn the heap only when dry or nearly so. Finally, deposit it in the border, and after the vines are planted, mulch it with two or three inches of half rotted leaves.

PLANTING AND TRAINING THE VINES.

   Take good, strong, two year old vines, grown from eyes, place them within sixteen inches of the front of the house, and two feet apart in the row. Set the vines close down to the young wood, and if from pots, cover the ball of earth and roots with about two inches of soil.
   If the planting be done in the fall, cut the vines down to two eyes, as soon as the leaves are off. Cover the vines with four to six inches of fine charcoal or litter, to protect from frost, and if litter be used as a cover look out for mice.
   In spring, it is advisable to retard the cold vinery, and keep the plants back as long as possible. As soon as safe from frost, or if you have the aid of a flue, or stoves, say about the first of April in the latitude of Philadelphia, uncover the vines and slightly stir the border. No manure is now needed, unless it be a small

quantity of special fertilizer, such as we have recommended in the section on that subject.

When the border is uncovered give it a thorough soaking of pure rain water.

As soon as the canes have broken two inches long, select the strongest bud, giving the preference to the one nearest the ground, and remove the other. The weather being mild, the canes will grow rapidly. Air the house freely in warm, mild weather, as soon as the thermometer reaches 55°, with top air only. Keep the border moderately moist, not wet, but when the border is watered, give it a good soaking. When the vines have grown two or three feet, and the temperature under glass has increased to 70°, put on one foot of air on the top of the house and keep the floor sprinkled with water, during sunny days, shutting up the house before the sun leaves it; at the same time thoroughly syringe all parts of the house, vines and all, night and morning, with pure, soft, warm rain water, which has been exposed to the sun in tubs, so as to be of the same temperature as the atmosphere in the house. Use a syringe with a fine rose, throwing a mere mist on the vines, and apply it gently, so as not to injure the delicate tissue of the leaves.

About the middle of May, if the weather be mild, admit about two inches of air on the top of the house about 8 o'clock in the evening, leaving it open all night all through the season, except in cold, chilly nights.

As the canes advance in growth, stop all laterals to

one joint, leaving one new leaf every time, till the vine reaches the top of the house, when the leader will be stopped,—and continue to stop in the same way, leaving one new leaf on each joint till the end of the season. The best length of rafter for a cold grapery is about fifteen feet.

After the first of September, give the border no more water. When the leaves fall, and the wood is well ripened, cut down every alternate cane within two eyes of the ground, and the canes intended to be fruited next year to the height of about six feet.

Late in the season, lay the canes down, and cover them up with charcoal or litter, as before directed, for winter protection.

FRUITING THE VINES.

About the first of April, uncover the vines and apply to the border a top dressing of such manures as you think best, or the special fertilizers which we have recommended in another part of this work. Then give the border a good soaking with pure, soft water. Bend the fruiting canes down in a half circle, by slinging them loosely along the lower wires, till the vines break two or three inches. Then tie up the canes perpendicularly. Two buds will usually appear at each joint. Remove the weaker bud, which is usually the lower one.

As soon as the vines are uncovered, in sunny days

syringe freely night and morning, with pure rain water. When the atmosphere of the house rises to 50° or 55°, give four or five inches of top ventilation, in clear days, increasing to one foot as the heat rises to 75° or 80°.

Apply small quantities of special fertilizers, from time to time, such as your experience suggests, or such as we recommend in our section on this subject.

The vines will now be coming into flower. Keep the house as warm as you can, with moderate ventilation, and maintain a high degree of humidity in the atmosphere, by sprinkling the floor and syringing the vines freely night and morning.

When the fruit shows, select the bunches nearest the main stem for preservation, stopping each shoot two joints beyond the bunch, and continue to stop in the same way, leaving one new leaf each time, which will cause a growth of strong, well developed foliage.

Thin the fruit on the bunches, immediately after it is set the size of a pin's head, on all free setting kinds, leaving not more than twenty per cent. of the fruit, and cutting out the berries from the inside so as to extend the size of the bunches as much as possible.

Now top dress pretty freely with special fertilizers, containing super-phosphate of lime and tartrate of potash, or whatever else your views of grape culture may deem most useful to assist in the formation of fruit.

Keep the border quite moist during the formation of fruit, and air freely during warm days, on the top of the house, with doors and bottom ventilation close. Let the whole house be frequently sprinkled, and keep the atmosphere very humid, and allow a little night ventilation, as advised for first season in growing canes.

As soon as the grapes begin to stone, cease stopping, and let the foliage ramble at will. When the fruit begins to color, admit a little front air on mild days, and very warm nights, and discontinue syringing and watering the border, as a dry house hastens the ripening process.

The *growing canes* will be treated in precisely the same way as the canes the first season after planting, stopping the laterals, as before described.

This completes the chief directions for managing the cold grapery under the renewal system, (growing the canes and fruiting,) for two seasons. The following years will be but a repetition of the same methods, except in respect to the size of the border, and the entire renewal of the vines.

After two seasons, it may be advisable to increase the width of the border from three to five feet, in order to allow the roots more space, and to present to them some fresh compost; this may be done by concreting the space intended to be covered by the new border; extend the atmospheric conductors, build up the brick work, and then add compost prepared as before. This same process may be repeated, from time to time, until the border is extended entirely across the house, if desired, thus giving fresh nutriment to the roots, in large bulk, of a simple natural character, as well as by top dressing with special fertilizers.

After some years, under this system, the main stem of the vines will become too long to be fruited with advantage, and the tip of the vines may then be layered, and fresh plants, with new roots, will be speedily produced to take the place of the old.

If desired, the whole house may be renovated, in this way, in a single season, and the greater part of the old border may be removed, after the new plants are fairly established, the old roots being taken out with the soil; and fresh compost may be introduced in place of the old, begining with a border only three feet wide as at first. Thus we have, under this system, a constant, never ending, renewal of wood, roots and border, from year to year, and from one period of time to another, as required by the condition of the vines, keeping the roots always near the surface of the earth, in a soil of well regulated temperature, and in every desirable respect under perfect control.

NOTE ON "STOPPING."—In stopping the laterals, as directed in this work, it will be understood that they are not to be kept shortened to one joint, but they are to be stopped once in three or four weeks, according to the rapidity of growth, making four or five stops in a season, and of course forming four or five joints on each lateral, leaving one new leaf on every joint each time of stopping.

The Hot-House.

THE renewal system of grape culture may be applied to the Hot-house in precisely the same way as to the vineyard and Cold Grapery. The design of this work does not permit us to give detailed instruction in the general management of the hot-house, and we shall therefore only say that in houses with very long rafters, say fifteen to twenty feet, the weaker kinds of grapes will not probably grow strong enough, upon this system, to fruit them the whole length of the rafter the first year or two, but they should be cut back in proportion to their strength. Some of the strong canes can be fruited the second season, half way up the house, say ten feet. Others, if weaker, should be cut back to four or six feet of fruiting wood. The second time of fruiting, the weaker vines can be extended to ten feet, and the third time the entire length of the rafter.

In small hot-houses, with a rafter only eight or ten feet long, the canes may be planted in the spring, and one-half of them (as before directed,) may be fruited the entire length of the rafter the second year. Small houses, with rafters only six or eight feet long, are the best size for early forcing.

Injurious effect of deep, rich Borders, and deep planting in Vineyards.

The "Ohio German System," and indeed all other systems of grape culture practised or advocated in this country, are based upon the plan of deep, rich borders, and deep trenching and heavy manuring for vineyards. Indeed, so far do some of the Ohio writers carry this doctrine, that they advise the cultivator to "cut off the roots of the vines near the *surface* of the ground, and for four or five inches below the surface, that the roots, while the vines are young, may be established at the proper depth;" that is, we presume, as deeply as possible. (See R. Buchanan on Grape Culture, pages 16, 17.) A more absurd or injurious practice could scarcely be conceived. We should rather advise that all roots which penetrate more than five inches below the surface should be cut off, and that *the surface roots be preserved.*

Mr. Reemelin, of Ohio, whose treatise on the vine is well known, seems to be a little dubious about the merits of the root-pruning practice above described. He says: "I doubt the propriety of going down so far and cutting off the roots. I have taken up many grape vines, from five to ten years old, and I can say, from practical experience, that those vines were the thriftiest upon whose stem not only the foot-roots, but the side-roots were in good condition." Mr. R. adds that he "considers it of first importance that the foot-roots should penetrate deeply."

In our opinion, deep borders and deep planting constitute two of the greatest errors now existing in grape culture. We think no border should be made more than two feet deep, and no vineyard soil should be made rich to a greater depth than eighteen inches, or trenched for any other purpose than to render it open and porous. No vine should be planted more than four to eight inches deep, and instead of making any effort to induce the roots to go down deeper than that, every effort should be made to keep them within four inches of the surface; and as soon as the roots are found to penetrate to the depth of three feet, we would advise the vine to be renewed by layers. We will guarantee that if a trial be made, near Cincinnati, where the grape rot prevails so badly, by planting the Catawba grape on the surface of a rock, in four inches of soil, and well mulched winter and summer, a good crop of grapes will be obtained, and that the rot will never be seen on a vine so planted— nor upon any other vine planted shallow, in a porous soil, and properly mulched.

It is frequently stated, by writers on grape culture, that in many parts of Europe they spade up the ground for vineyards, from two to five feet deep. Mr. Reemelin, of Ohio, says so in his Vine Dresser's Manual. This may be true, in some instances, but if true, it does not by any means prove that it is best to induce the vines to root so deeply. It cannot, however, be the general custom, for two reasons; first, the people in Spain, and some other countries, are too indolent and too poor to expend so much labor on the preparation of the vineyard; and secondly, the nature of the rocky soil on the hill-sides, where most of the vineyards are located, does not admit of such deep culture. Mr. Redding, whose treatise on Modern Wines is a standard English authority on this subject, says, that at Malaga, in Spain, where the most delicious wine is produced, " most of the vines flourish in about eighteen inches of a rich loam or mould, upon a blue shaly substratum, or rocky formation. The vineyards are, many of them, situated at a great height above the sea, where the earth about the vines *must be carefully secured*," (so little is there of it, and so loosely does it lie on the rocks, we presume.) Redding, in his interesting treatise, gives many other instances of shallow soils which produce large crops of grapes, and the best of wine.

The effect of a deep, rich border in the vinery, for the first two or three years, is very gratifying to the cultivator. The first year the vine makes a strong, rampant growth, and fine foliage, and continues to grow in this luxuriant way for two years longer. The owner of the vines, and the gardener, are delighted with their success. The border is deep, and rich, and the vines are truly magnificent. Such a border as that cannot assuredly give out, for it gets more rich food every year, and vines of such luxuriance certainly cannot meet with check or disaster. So they reason.

But sometimes in the third year, they begin to discover that there is something the matter with the vines. The bunches are large, the berries are large, but the foliage begins to decline a little, and the fruit does not color quite so well as usual.

The next year or two, the vines continue to produce large wood, but they break in the spring badly, the wood being immature, and are much subject to mildew. The roots have now penetrated too deeply to maintain a healthy relation to the top of the vine.

In the fifth year the fruit sometimes scarcely colors at all; the berries remain red, and a great portion of them shank.

During the sixth and seventh years, the vines in deep, rich borders begin to decline very rapidly. The leaves, instead of being, as before, a foot or fifteen inches in diameter, will often be seen no larger than maple leaves; and thus the work of destruction goes on till the eighth and ninth years, (when the vines, if properly managed, ought to be in the greatest perfection,) and then, as we often see in deep borders, they nearly die out, and become entirely useless. This is the history of such borders, and of deep planting, in vineries all around Philadelphia.

In contrast to this common system of culture, we will present an experiment tried by Mr. Fleming, of England, a well known grape grower, to resuscitate one of these decaying vineries, deeply planted in a rich, deep border, as published in the Gardener's Chronicle.

Mr. Fleming had the care of a vinery, which was much subject to mildew; the grapes never colored well; the leaves were small and burnt; the grapes did not mature.

This ill success was, at first, attributed to the old crown glass, with which the house was covered. This glass was removed, and the house was glazed with the best horticultural sheet glass, rolled, to destroy the focus, but with no good result. They then put on a ridge and furrow roof, but with no perceptible improvement in the condition of the vines. It was at last conceded that the defect must be in the border.

Mr. Fleming then commenced at the foot of the house, and very carefully took out all the soil and roots, down to the drainage; and as he raised the roots of the vines, tied them up in damp moss, and suspended them from the front of the house. He thus entirely removed the old border, and all the roots of the vines; re-concreted the bottom of the border; laid a new drainage, well secured; put in a fresh border, not very rich, but chiefly composed of fresh, virgin soil, with a little bone dust and well rotted manure; spread out the roots of the vines upon the surface of the border, and covered them with two inches of soil, well mulched.

Now mark the result. This experiment was performed late in September, after a crop had been taken off. The vines were in leaf, and the leaves scarcely flagged during the whole operation, although the vines were not cut back any more than they would have been if not lifted, but were pruned in the usual way, and allowed to fruit the next season, the whole length of the canes. The vines broke rather weak, about as they had done for some years previously, but increased in substance and strength rapidly before the bunches appeared; the bunches elongated to an enormous size, and the vines perfected a crop of grapes which took the first premium at the fall exhibition in the Crystal Palace at Sydenham, against all the best vineries in Great Britain! So much for shallow planting in a border moderately rich. We feel sure that this is the best practice, and that gardeners everywhere must sooner or later come to it, and all vine-growers also, both in-doors and out.

The reason why vines do not thrive for a number of years, in deep borders, is this: it is impossible to preserve an equal degree of temperature, and an equal action, between the roots and the tops of the canes. For instance, the tops of the canes start early in the spring, both in the vineyard and in the vinery, long before the soil or the border becomes warmed to the depth of two or three feet, and before the roots are properly excited into action, and hence a great draught is made upon the resources of the vine before it is properly supplied with sap. Again, in the fall, the action of the roots, excited by the warmth of the soil or border, continues long after the tops ought to be at rest, and a late growth of succulent, immature wood, is the result. Where the roots of vines extend from a hot-house into a deep outside border, the effect is even worse than in the vineyard. In all cases, however, deep planting will produce rot, mildew, shanking, and final destruction of the vines.

Special Manures for the Grape.

BRIGHT'S GRAPE FERTILIZER.

The grape delights, most of all, in a limestone soil. The best wine grapes grown in Europe, have been produced on artificial terraces or borders, on the hill-side ledges of limestone rocks. *Lime* is, indeed, required in abundance by almost all fruit producing plants and trees. A good method of using lime, where it is not sufficiently abundant in the soil, is to apply twenty or thirty bushels annually per acre, and it is more efficient if this quantity be distributed in small portions of say three to five bushels at a time, before rain, at intervals of several weeks, throughout the year. Or, it may be used upon sod and peat, when preparing composts, before the addition of stable manure, or other ammoniacal substances.

The next special manure required by the grape is *ammonia*, or nitrogenous matter. The grape is generally declared to be a gross feeder; it is thought to require a large amount of rich manure. This idea is in the main correct, but not to the extent that was former supposed. The old plan of manuring grape borde and arbors, by burying the carcasses of animals, slaughter-house offal, hog manure, and other material of a similar character under the roots of vines, is now, we presume abandoned by all intelligent persons who have kept pace with the progress in horticulture. Even bone-dust is not now placed beneath the roots, though it may be, to some extent, mixed with the soil of borders and vineyards. But as to nitrogenous compounds, stable manure, slaughter-house offal, guano, &c., it is better that they should not be mixed largely with the soil, in planting a vineyard, unless it be very poor, nor indeed should they be thus applied around or beneath the roots of any fruit-bearing plant or tree, at the time of planting.

The grape requires ammonia, or ammoniacal manures, such as we have mentioned, but they should be applied late in the fall in the vineyard, or in early spring, as we have directed for pot culture. You may manure your vineyard annually, in the fall, as you would a field of wheat, and fork it into the soil; or you may mix the ammoniacal substance in your special compost, as we have done in the Grape Fertilizer.

After ammonia, comes *phosphoric acid*, or *phosphate of lime*, as a special manure for the grape. This should be, not in the form of crude bones, or bone-earth, or bone-dust, but in the form of soluble super-phosphate of lime. Vast sums of money have been wasted by the application of crude bones and bone-dust to vineyards. Even finely ground bones will scarcely decompose and yield up their phosphoric acid to the grape roots in the life-time of man, while in the soluble form the valuable constituent of bones, the phosphoric acid, becomes entirely available the first season.

The fourth important inorganic element of the grape vine and its fruit, is *potash*, in various combinations, as silicate of potash, nitrate of potash, tartrate of potash, carbonate of potash, &c. Potash should, we presume, be placed first and highest on the list, and the others in the inverse order as noticed, viz: first potash, then phosphoric acid, ammonia, lime. Soda, or soda ash, may perhaps in some instances, serve the purpose of potash, though it does not enter largely into the composition of the vine or the grape.

The *acids* also play an important part in the formation of the grape, such as the tartaric, malic, carbonic, silicic, nitric, sulphuric and tannic acids.

The starchy and saccharine elements and compounds, produced by the bases and acids, have also to be considered in our views of grape culture.

Lime and potash enter largely into the composition of the wood, ammonia stimulates the growth of foliage, the phosphoric acid promotes the tendency to fruit, potash develops fruit juices, carbonic and tartaric acids elaborate sweetness and rich vinous flavor, and all these substances, and more which it is unnecessary to name, as they are found in all good soils, under the combined influence of light, heat, and moisture, produce the perfect fruit.

To instruct the public at large as to the best method

of obtaining and using all these necessary constituents of the grape, in a brief hand-book like this, has seemed to us almost a hopeless task. It would require at least a complete elementary treatise on the chemistry of the substances named, which few would read, unless previously instructed in chemistry, and still fewer would understand, or attempt to follow. There is nothing of which the purely practical man is more justly doubtful than his ability even to use potash, or any other simple chemical agent, with safety and success in the preparation of manure.

With these views, and by the urgent request of numerous friends, we have prepared a *Grape Fertilizer* for popular use, containing all the ingredients necessary to grow and fruit the grape, in pots, in the hot-house, in the garden, upon the trellis, and in the vineyard: precisely that compost or combination of agents, which we have ourselves so successfully employed for years in the growing of grapes, only more perfectly made, and more scientifically combined, than we have usually made it for our own use.

People who have visited our grapery have often asked us "What manures do you use to make your grapes grow so finely, and fruit so heavily?" It was impossible to answer this question within the limits of a brief conversation, and hence many have thought us very secret and selfish in our grape culture. This is not so. We have been willing to explain the whole art, and here publish it; but we are quite convinced, that unless the special manures required by the grape are provided in a convenient and perfect form, few persons among the thousands who may read this work, would be able to attain the highest degree of success in grape culture.

Stable manure, or even slaughter-house manure, alone, will not grow and perfect the best fruit, nor the best crop, although it may produce immense canes. We advise the use of some stable manure, or other rich manure of like character, or of guano; but we feel assured that in really good soil a first rate crop of fine grapes may be produced without any stable manure, guano, or other stimulating manure whatever, by the use of the chemical elements of the grape above described, which form the ingredients of our fertilizer. Most persons have no doubt noticed that grape vines and fruit trees, in good soil, usually *grow*, that is increase in size, and length of branches, and abundance of foliage, well enough, without stable or other common manure,—but *they don't fruit*. Now soap suds, containing carbonic acid and potash, applied to an old unfruitful vine, or tree, will often cause it to fruit abundantly. The vine may obtain carbonic acid, and ammonia, from the atmosphere, and may grow finely, but if the inorganic or chemical substances required to produce fruit, be exhausted from the soil, they can only be supplied by the application of compounds containing them.

The Grape Fertilizer which we present to the public, is intended chiefly for popular use. The scientific man will of course know what chemical agents to use, in grape culture, and how to use them, and will not come to us for instruction, though he may not decline a hint from us, when sustained by successful practice. To the gentleman, however, who does not study horticulture, and whose gardener does not understand chemistry, we believe a well prepared Grape Fertilizer, at a low price, adapted to the grapery and trellis, will prove a valuable acquisition, as it may save him much time, expense, and probably serious failure in the efforts of his gardener to attain a high point in grape culture. To the amateur grape-grower, in small gardens and vineyards, and to the owner of a single vine or arbor of vines, it will be exceedingly useful and convenient. We have long had special manures for corn and wheat, and why not for grapes? The latter is indeed more imperatively demanded than the former, because the art of selecting and mixing the necessary ingredients is less generally known, and hence greater mistakes are liable to be made in any attempts to accomplish it.

The Grape Fertilizer which we have prepared, contains all the ingredients necessary to grow and fruit the grape, in abundance, except carbonic acid, or carbonaceous matter. Well rotted sod, peat sweetened with lime, or rotted straw, and well rotted stable manure will supply carbon.

The Grape Fertilizer contains ammonia, phosphoric acid, potash, salts of lime and soda, iron, &c., &c., all the inorganic elements of vine and fruit, in proper combination with vegetable acids, especially the tartaric acid.

Tartaric Acid we have found, in a free state, the most useful of all the special manures for the grape. The fact that the lees of wine, or grape juice, deposits large quantities of tartaric acid, or bi-tartrate of potash, (cream of tartar,) has long been known to the world, and yet grape growers have for centuries been blind to the importance of this substance in grape culture. Not till after we had experimented with the use of tartaric acid, and tartrate of potash, could we feel certain that we had the culture and fruiting of the grape perfectly under our control. Sometimes we succeeded, and sometimes we failed, nor could we discover the cause. One day, in reading some scientific work, our attention was called to the fact, that nearly all the cream of tartar of commerce, was obtained from the lees of wine. New light at once broke into our mind. Here, it was evident, was an important acid, necessary to the perfection of the grape, entirely overlooked. We commenced experimenting at once, with tartaric acid, adding it to our compost heaps and using it in a variety of ways and a variety of combinations. At last we hit upon the right union with potash and other substances, and we have never since been at loss to fruit a healthy vine as heavily as it could bear. In fact, our vines fruited too heavily, and we immediately commenced the dwarfing system, and the growing of larger bunches of finer quality, which is the truest and highest point of the art.

Our Grape Fertilizer is an ammoniated compound of phosphate and tartrate of potash and lime, or more preperly speaking it is a compound of ammonia and superphosphate of lime, and tartrate of potash, in a form sufficiently soluble to meet the wants of the grape vine. If required, it will all be available in a single season, but if not taken up by the vines, it will remain in any good soil for years, until it is taken up by plants, and cannot be washed out by rains, or evaporated by heat. It is ready for use, yet enduring as the earth itself. Being manufactured on a large scale, it can be sold cheaper than it can be made by any single individual purchasing the ingredients in small quantities and working without proper apparatus, even if he possess the requisite scientific skill to make the proper combinations. We believe it will be of immense service to grape growers, and save them a vast amount of trouble, expense and disappointment, in their efforts to grow the grape by the use of ordinary manures.

The Grape Fertilizer may be applied to the vine in pots, in the field or garden, as a top dressing, in the fall, after the vine has ceased growing, in the spring, and during the summer when undergoing the stoning process when the fruit ceases to swell for a time, and in addition to growing a fine crop of grapes, it will perfect the fruit a week or two earlier than if not so fertilized.

The Grape Fertilizer will be furnished in large and small packages, adapted to the wants of grape growers, and detailed directions will accompany each package as to method of using, quantity per acre, or per vine.

Method of applying our Grape Fertilizer.

The Grape Fertilizer which we present to the public should be applied to vines frequently, at various seasons of the year, in small quantities, as parts of it are volatile and might be lost before being taken up by the roots, if the whole quantity intended for one season were applied all at once.

As soon as the foliage falls off in autumn, the vines should receive a dressing of fertilizing agents, in order that these substances may pass into the soil and enter into chemical combination with its particles during the winter, and promote new chemical conditions in the soil itself. When the vines start in the spring, a fresh dressing should be given, and during the spring, while the rain is falling freely, slight sprinklings of Fertilizer should be frequently thrown around the roots, to be dissolved and carried into the soil at once by the water. And again, in summer, when the fruit is stoning, and the vines seem to be in a partial state of rest, a free dose of Fertilizer should be given during rainy weather, to assist in perfecting the grapes.

To a poor soil, in which there is a scanty supply of the salts of lime and potash, and but little ammonia or phosphoric acid, the Fertilizer may be applied at the rate of one ton per acre, the first season, and say, six hundred pounds the second and following seasons, though three hundred pounds on a first rate soil will show a marked and profitable effect. For single vines, or vines on arbors, from a peck to a bushel may be applied in a season, to each vine, or even two bushels may be used on old vines which have had but little special manure for many years, if it be widely spread over the surface of the ground, say upon a space ten or fifteen feet square and carefully worked into the top soil, in divided quantities, at different seasons of the year, as before directed. Indeed, if any one should wish to try the experiment, upon a large old vine, we think that as much as four or six bushels might be applied to a single old vine, of large size, with safety, especially if mixed for two or three weeks with one or two cart-loads of muck or wet sod from an old meadow, and turned two or three times before using it. The caustic ingredients of the Fertilizer would thus be partially neutralized by the muck or sod, and also absorbed, so that the action of its ingredients would not be expended all at once, or too speedily upon the vine. All large applications of Fertilizer for the restoration of old vines, should of course be made late in the fall, and in early spring, and not during the growing season.

For pot vines of one year old or less, only slight

sprinklings will be required, say a pint or so in a season. Two year old and fruiting vines may be top-dressed with one or two quarts during the year, the old material being removed occasionally and fresh applied, as may seem to be required. The heaviest dressings should be made late in the fall, and the first thing in the spring before the vines have started. It will always be well to apply to the pots a little fresh soil before giving the Fertilizer, and this again may be covered with soil, or leaf mould, with much advantage. So in making applications of Fertilizer to out of door vines, a mulching or dressing of good soil or leaf mould over the special manure will be highly useful.

Our Fertilizer is quite as powerful as guano in respect to the quantity and value of its ingredients, but it is not so volatile, soluble, or caustic, and hence acts more slowly, lasts longer, and is not so dangerous to plants. It contains all the special manures required by the grape for the growth of wood and the production of fruit, and will be found exceedingly convenient for those who do not care to trouble themselves about making composts of crude and offensive substances in order to obtain the necessary fertilizing agents.

APPENDIX.

Inside Borders—Shallow Planting.

THE views presented in this work, in respect to the construction of vine borders and shallow planting, may seem to demand some defence and explanation beyond what is contained in the body of the essay. We consider the positions assumed, and the practice advised, highly important to fruit growers, and we can show that although seemingly new, and esteemed by many good cultivators of questionable merit, they are really endorsed by several of the leading horticultural writers in the United States.

The practice of deep planting and heavy manuring, for fruit trees and grape vines, was first brought into active use, in this country, by A. J. DOWNING, who, with all his great merits as a writer on horticultural topics, has been the means of destroying many thousands of trees and vines by his directions for planting. When we use the expression "deep planting," we do not always mean setting the tree too deep at first, but we mean so digging and manuring the soil under the tree as to invite its roots immediately and deeply down into the sub-soil. What we desire is, to keep the roots of trees and vines, as much as possible, near the surface.

These opinions we first presented to the public, in an article on Dwarf Pear culture, in the *Gardener's Monthly*, for March, 1859, in reply to an article by Mr. E. Norton of Connecticut, in the Horticulturist. We noticed Mr. Norton's article because his planting was made upon the old Downing plan, which has been in general use, among amateurs at least. We quote such portions of the article alluded to, as bear immediately upon the question at issue.

PEAR TREES ON QUINCE STOCK.

BY WILLIAM BRIGHT.

The article by Mr. E. Norton in the Horticulturist for December last, on the general failure of the Pear on Quince Stock, has induced me to present you with a few suggestions upon this subject which I think may prove useful to persons who may hereafter attempt the culture of the pear especially upon quince roots. Mr. Norton's remarks are very fair and apparently well considered, the result of much personal experience and careful observation. But they contain within themselves, in my opinion, the evidence of erroneous views of pear culture, which are very common, and to which, in a great measure, the ill success of dwarf pears may be attributed.

Mr. Norton says he planted four hundred quince-rooted pear trees, thus: " Holes were dug *two and-a-half feet deep* by three or four wide, and *filled with a carefully prepared compost*, not too rich, but having all the ingredients prescribed by the experts." The manner in which the trees were set out, in my opinion, presents the one great fatal error in the planting of fruit trees, which runs through all the works upon this subject, and prevails in practice to an extent sufficient to account for at least half the misfortunes of fruit-growers.

The great cardinal principle in all fruit culture, and in the case of the dwarf pear in particular, should be to keep the roots as near the surface of the earth as possible, and not to invite them down to a depth of three feet, by the use of rich composts. They will go down rapidly enough, and far enough, be sure of that, if the ground is well ploughed; but we ought not to encourage them to go down; and to this end, we should place the manure upon the surface of the ground, rather than under them. The recent experiments in surface manuring, in England and America, prove conclusively that, for most purposes, this is really the best plan, and that there is very little loss of valuable material occasioned by the exposure of the manure to the atmosphere, whether decomposed or not. But there is even a stronger reason for the method of manuring which I recommend. If the roots of pear trees are induced to go a long way down into the subsoil, the buds and leaves will start in the spring before the earth is so far warmed by solar heat as to excite the roots into full action, and thus a heavy draft must be made upon the vitality of the tree, by the growing foliage, before the sap begins to ascend with sufficient rapidity to meet this demand. Again, in the fall, when the earth is warmer than the atmosphere, the roots will continue too long in an active state, thus producing a succulent growth of wood late in the season, long after the whole tree ought to be in a state of repose, in order to ripen its wood. Leaf-blight in the first case, and frozen sap blight in the other, must be the inevitable consequence of such a condition of the tree. This is a principle of the highest consequence in the management of fruit trees, grape vines, &c. I plant all fruit trees as shallow as possible, having due regard to the natural requirements of the tree.

Mr. Norton says he "filled" the holes dug for his trees with "carefully prepared compost, having all the ingredients prescribed by experts." Now, the common advice of the books on fruit culture is, to use for such composts sod, loam, raw and ground bones, ashes, plaster, slaughter-house offal, night-soil, stable manure, &c. Mr. Norton writes like an intelligent man, and therefore we will not suspect him of using a mass of strong rich nitrogenous matter and alkalies, sufficient to kill any tree at once; and, indeed, he declares that the compost was "not too rich." But if he placed under his trees "all the ingredients prescribed by experts," even in moderation, in my opinion, he committed a grave error. A transplanted fruit tree should never, I think, be placed either *in* or *upon* such a compost, or any other manuring substance. The soil should be well pulverized, and the tree should be planted at the proper depth in the simple, natural, good top soil or loam, and covered with simple mild loam only. No manure should be placed under it, none over it (at first,) and none nearer than from four to six inches from it on the sides.

"The transplanted tree," says Mr. Jacob Seneff, a highly successful pear-grower of this city, "is like a child, convalescent from some severe injury. It must not be fed at once with stimulants; it must have time to recover itself gradually by nature's own processes, before you give it rich and abundant food." There is much good sense in this remark. To say nothing of the probability that you may destroy the tree by the excess of putrescent matter, and the powerful chemical action of your composts, when holes two and a half feet deep are filled with "all the ingredients prescribed by experts," it is evident that a young transplanted tree needs no such material to help its growth for several months, or for the first year. The best compost for a newly planted tree is precisely that from which it was taken— the simple, natural loam, well enriched by previous cultivation. This is all it wants to assist it in getting started in its new residence; this is nearly all it will bear without injury.

The holes for pear trees on quince stocks, in my opinion, should be dug only deep enough to set the tree so that the union of the graft shall be covered an inch or so with the natural soil. Put no manure of any kind under or over them. You may, if you please, place a little compost in the open cavity, as you are filling it up, six inches from them, but even this is not necessary. You can feed them soon enough and amply enough by top-dressing at the proper time, and the manure will be all the better for going down in a state of solution, instead of being placed around the roots in the form of gross and powerful composts.

The haste to manure transplanted fruit trees is not only a great injury, but an unnecessary and useless expense; and the cost of it, as advised by "the experts," prevents a great many persons from engaging in fruit culture. The very excellent and elegant treatise on Pear Culture by Mr. Thomas W. Field, the intelligent Secretary of the American Pomological Society, recommends a plan of trenching and manuring as a necessary preparation for the pear orchard, which, I think, will not only have a tendency to deter many persons from engaging in pear culture, but, if followed, will cause many who adopt it to form a very ill opinion of the dwarf pear. Mr. Field says, to attain the highest success, you must trench the whole ground three feet deep with the spade, mixing in the process the entire top soil and subsoil to that depth, and incorporating with the whole fifty two-horse loads of stable-manure per acre. Not only so, but he advises well-rotted stable-manure to be placed in the holes when the trees are planted, and more manure to be sprinkled in as the holes are filled up, only taking care not to allow the manure to come in contact with the roots! Now, to say nothing of the fact that stable-manure alone is not the best manure for fruit trees, the cost of trenching an acre of land upon this plan, he admits, will be $100. Fifty two-horse loads of stable-manure will cost, six miles from Philadelphia, from $250 to $300. Four hundred good dwarf pear trees for an acre, with labor of planting, &c., will cost at least $200; thus making the first outlay for an acre of trees, from $550 to $600. This, with the value of the land, after-culture, and risk, is rather too high a figure to render the culture of dwarf pears, "for market purposes," an inviting speculation.

Now, the truth is, a soil suitable for a pear orchard may be thoroughly prepared with the sub-soil plough, by cross-ploughing, at about the cost of four ordinary ploughings and two harrowings. This will give a soil eighteen inches in depth, well pulverized, which is ample. No general manuring is required; and, if done, will be a great waste of means. In all other respects, except that noticed, Mr. Field's book is a good one, and exhibits, on the part of its author, not only much literary skill, but a highly refined and susceptible nature.

For myself, I believe that the pear on the quince stock, if planted, as I have suggested, in the simple loam of a proper soil, well ploughed and sub-soiled, in a sheltered situation and proper exposure, and afterwards mulched, and top-dressed with proper manures, and properly pruned, and moderately fruited, will exhibit a degree of success far beyond that reported by Messrs. Allen, Norton and others, in all the middle and seaboard States of the Union, and will reward its cultivators with luscious and profitable harvests for a satisfactory number of years.

For the sake of the cause, we must be excused for bringing T. W. FIELD, Esq., forward to testify in favor of our views on this subject. He has shown such a noble and generous spirit, in this matter, that we feel confident of his forgiveness. In the *Gardener's Monthly* for May, 1859, may be found an article from which we quote the following passages:

PEAR CULTURE.

BY T. W. FIELD, NEW YORK.

The communication from Mr. Bright is conceived in so kindly a spirit of criticism, and written with so much intelligence, that I cannot allow him to retain a misapprehension upon the subject, nor omit to confess that there is just grounds for his stricture upon the article on Trenching and Manuring in Pear Culture.

I have not hitherto noticed any of the critiques upon my *brochure*, for several reasons; principally because I was heartily tired of writing upon the subject, but occasionally, because they were ill-natured, or written by those who had little interest in the subject. To Mr. Bright let me say, that he has given me the first misgivings upon the policy of what I had written, and that I confess his view to be the most philosophical regarding pear culture.

Still I must do myself the justice to say, that the great expense I recommended was qualified in several places in the book, by stating that it was the extreme of high cultivation, and that I felt it necessary to explain the processes by which the very highest result could be reached.

On those wretchedly light soils which it has been my fortune to cultivate, much less labor would scarcely secure success.

We have since learned that Mr. Field planted his pear trees on some city lots, which had been filled up with poor soil and rubbish, and that it was necessary for him to manure heavily, to bring the soil into a fertile condition. His own practice was no doubt correct, but the advice in his book was too much after the old Downing method, and was certainly not judicious. We are all too much in the habit of supposing that the practice which proves successful on any particular piece of soil, will be suited to all soils. We do not wish to punish Mr. Field for his want of reflection; we only desire to put the Secretary of the American Pomological Society, where he has voluntarily placed himself, on our side, in this discussion.

The Hon. Marshall P. Wilder, President of the American Pomological Society, after all his talk about "high culture," for the pear, still holds a position very similar to that which we advocate. We quote from the Report of the Pomological Lectures at New Haven, published in the *Gardener's Monthly*. After Mr. Wilder's lecture on the pear—" A member called in question the propriety of 'high culture' (as generally understood) for the pear on good soils, or the free manuring of the pear tree, and especially dwarf pears, with stable manure, as might be supposed necessary from the remarks of Mr. Wilder. This, he contended, was not practised by the most successful cultivators where the soil is good. Mr. Wilder not being present, it was explained by a friend, that he did not intend to say that the pear should be freely manured with stable manure on good soils, as he does on the poor, thin, gravelly soil of Dorchester; and in proof of this, a passage was quoted from his lecture, as follows: 'Surely it would be unwise to apply the same cultivation to the peach and the cherry as to the apple and the pear, or to treat any of these on new and fertile ground as in old and exhausted land.'

"The subject of deep and shallow planting, especially in its application to the pear, came up in this same discussion, and was pretty freely ventilated. The result of it was, a very general impression that pears, and especially the quince-rooted trees, have been planted too deeply, and that their roots should, if possible, be kept out of the subsoil. To do this, the pear must be budded low upon the quince stock, and the main root must be shortened as much as possible when set out; and in some instances it is better to make a slight concave mound around them with soil, (in order to cover the quince stock completely,) rather than to set them too deep in the ground. Much valuable information upon these topics was elicited from Mr. Barry, the distinguished nurseryman of Rochester, N. Y., who was in favor of a moderate depth in planting the dwarf pear, (always keeping the quince root entirely covered,) and of manuring only with well decomposed muck and manure compost, and not with fresh, highly stimulating stable manure."

P. BARRY, Esq., of Rochester, N. Y., in his lectures at New Haven, on the nursery and orchard management of fruit trees, presented views which well accord with our own, upon the subject of planting. We quote from the correspondence of the *Gardener's Monthly*:

"Mr. Barry advocated the preparation of the soil for the nursery and orchard, by ploughing and subsoiling to the depth of eighteen inches, and cross-ploughing and subsoiling when necessary, (and under-draining, if needed,) as amply sufficient in good soils, without trenching and turning up the subsoil three feet deep, as some have recommended. He also opposed very deep planting, and the use of highly stimulating manures, for pear trees on good soils. He manures his own pear trees with old compost of peat and manure every year, applying it in the fall."

Thomas Meehan, Esq., the talented and highly practical editor of the *Gardener's Monthly* also endorses our views on the necessity of keeping the roots of fruit trees and vines as near the surface of the ground as possible, as will be seen by the remarks which he appended to our article on the shallow planting of trees, which we take the liberty to insert in this Appendix.

P. B. Mead, Esq., the present editor of the *Horticulturist*, in a valuable article on the causes of pear blight, in the number for February, 1860, gives the result of fifteen years' experience in pear culture, proving that deep planting is fatal to the dwarf pear, while under what may be called surface planting, the trees were successful.

Here, then, we have the President and Secretary of the American Pomological Society, the editors of the two leading horticultural journals in America, and the principal nurseryman in the Union, all expressing views similar to our own, on the evils of deep planting and heavy manuring for fruit trees; and we think we may therefore fairly claim, that if we are considered by some persons a little radical in our positions, we are not, at any rate, a positive pomological heretic.

We now copy from the *Gardener's Monthly*, one of

our articles on shallow planting, as it has a direct bearing upon the principles advocated in this work; and also an article from the same journal, on the inside and divided border, for the vinery, which being stated in words different from those employed in this essay, may assist the reader to comprehend the construction of the new border.

Shallow Planting of Trees; Merits of the Practice.

BY WILLIAM BRIGHT.

It has been our custom for many years, in planting trees of all kinds—evergreens, ornamental and fruit trees—to set them as near the surface of the ground as possible, often exciting much alarm for the safety of the trees in the minds of anxious amateurs, and much contempt on the part of incipient gardeners, for the seeming absurdity of the practice. But having somehow got the idea into our head that this method of planting trees was the *true natural method*, we obstinately persevered in it, and now, after more than ten years' experience in the practice, it has grown into a settled system with us, and we have begun to find out the reasons why it is really the best and most judicious plan of planting trees.

In transplanting good specimens of evergreens, we usually endeavor to lift them with a ball of earth attached to the roots, fifteen or eighteen inches deep, and two feet or more in diameter. For such a tree, we make a hole only four inches deep, setting it, in fact almost on the surface of the ground. Then we throw about it one or two cart loads of good loam, working it up into a sort of mound, of a *concave* or crescent form, sloping off to a distance of six feet from the tree on all sides. After this we mulch the whole mound very heavily with leaf mould, or old litter, and keep it so mulched, winter and summer, for two years. The mulch must be heavy enough to keep the mound constantly moist in summer, and to keep out frost in winter.

Deciduous trees we plant in the same way, as near the surface as possible, and rarely dig a hole over four to six inches deep. If the bottom roots are too long, we shorten them. In setting the tree, we spread out the roots on every side, so as to form a natural support to the tree, in the same way that the ropes or guys support a derrick. The same rule of planting we apply, as nearly as possible, to fruit trees, though it is often difficult to do this with some of the stock obtained from the common nurseries. A great mistake is made by some nurserymen in working pears on the quince; they almost always work them too high on the stem. If budded as low as they ought to be, (right down on the crown of the quince root,) they could be planted shallow much more successfully; it would enable us to cover the bud with two or three inches of soil, without being compelled to plunge the roots deep into the cold and sterile sub-soil.

And here let us say, that in setting out deciduous ornamental trees, and standard fruit trees, after the method here described, it is necessary to pay particular attention to the fact that the roots must be spread out horizontally, at right angles to the tree, no matter how tough they may be, or how difficult it may seem to do this. If the tree be set with the roots extending perpendicularly downward, as they usually come from the nursery, it will be impossible to plant in shallow holes, as the tree would project too far out of the ground. The tree must not be set in the soil like a broom, but rather with its roots spread out precisely like a chicken's foot, with the toes extended at right angles from the leg. In this position it must be held firmly down till covered heavily with soil, when it will remain in place. The roots will then have the right direction for extending into the adjacent top soil.

For all kinds of trees we like to have the soil thoroughly and deeply ploughed and subsoiled; but the method of planting here recommended, renders deep trenching, and heavy manuring, and underdraining, in a majority of instances, quite unnecessary. Indeed, if we were to plant a fruit garden and lawn for ourselves, to-day, we would rather have all the trees set only two to four inches deep, in the decently good loam of a tolerably porous soil, (say a fair corn-field,) which had been subsoiled fifteen inches deep, without a particle of manure, than to have a field trenched three feet deep, and manured at the rate of two hundred horse-loads of manure to the acre, if the trees were to be set in the usual way, in deep holes dug for the purpose, so as to

APPENDIX. 109

force or invite the main roots two or three feet downwards into the ungenial subsoil.

Our chief reasons for this shallow planting are these: it is nature's own method of growing trees, and experience has proved to us that man has never devised a better. In the forest and field, wherever trees grow naturally, you will always find the largest number of roots just under the surface of the earth, in the top soil. Few or no roots, except the tap roots, extend downwards very deeply, but in the forest they run along for an immense distance just under the *mulching of leaves*, which both feed and protect them. A common loamy soil is only about six or eight inches deep, and this is all the material there really is in a field in a condition to furnish food for trees. Now, if you set a tree very near the surface of the ground, the roots will extend rapidly, freely and widely in the good top soil, and there they find their appropriate nutriment. If the light is excluded by mulching, as is done in the forest by leaves, you have all the conditions necessary for chemical changes in the soil, and *root feeding*, viz: heat, moisture and darkness; and no crude, cold, sour, uncongenial particles of matter to obstruct or poison the roots. Decomposition is constantly going on in the surface soil, and this is materially aided by *plant life*, which vegetable physiologists tell us acts like a ferment in dough, or like lime in muck, setting up chemical changes in the soil, which go on afterwards to an almost unlimited extent.

A surface-planted tree is placed in its *natural element*, a well decomposed and rapidly changing soil. Its roots get plenty of air, and if well mulched, are always moist; they become like the body and branches of the tree itself, accustomed to changes of temperature, and in the fall *ripen and harden off their wood* almost in the same way that a grape vine does its branches. But still the roots of a well mulched tree are never so liable to be affected by frost as even a deeply planted tree, for you will frequently find in the forest, under a heavy covering of leaves, in winter, that the frost has only penetrated to the depth of two inches, when in exposed ground the soil is frosted to the depth of four feet.

A surface-planted tree, immediately fed with one or two cart-loads of good loam, placed around the cut ends of its roots, and well mulched, is in a much more favorable condition to live and thrive, than a tree plunged deeply down into a cold, dank cistern of a hole, even if supplied with abundance of manure, and all sorts of special fertilizers. The surface-planted tree can and will send out its roots far and wide in the adjacent surface-soil; but the deeply planted tree finds nothing congenial or inviting in the soil around its roots, even if that soil be so well trenched or sub-soiled that it is able to penetrate it. A very large proportion of all the failures which have been made in growing fruit trees, and especially the pear, are to be attributed, in our opinion, to deep planting and excessive manuring. Nature shows us plainly what to do: plant shallow, give all manures in light and frequent doses, and protect the roots from sun and frost by mulching.

As evidence of the practical merit of the plan of surface-planting which we advocate, we will take the liberty to refer to the magnificent specimens of Norway Spruce, Austrian Pine, and other evergreens, on the lawn of J. S. Lovering, Esq., of Oak Hill, on Old York Road, near Philadelphia, which we planted upon this system. These fine trees were about four feet, and four feet six inches high when planted. They were taken up with balls of earth about eighteen inches deep and two feet in diameter, and set on the surface of the lawn in cavities not more than three or four inches deep; mounds were formed around them with good loam, and they were mulched for two years as before described. They never met with any check or injury; the foliage never suffered in the least; and they are now, when only six years planted, the finest of specimen trees, upwards of eighteen and twenty feet high, the admiration of every beholder competent to judge of their excellence and beauty.

The same may be said of the evergreens which we planted five years ago on the grounds of J. Swift, Esq., half a mile north of Mr. Lovering, on the York Road, in a very exposed, bleak situation. Here, where the white pine deeply planted, turned brown and lost its foliage in winter, the Austrians, shallow planted, not only endured the fierce north-westers without injury, but always made a fine growth, and retained, under all circumstances, their rich native luxuriance.

There are other lawns in our immediate vicinity, where we have planted evergreens, and all sorts of delicate deciduous trees, in September and November, upon this system of shallow beds, with moun's and mulching, without losing one tree in a thousand, and with a degree of success in the growth and beauty of the trees, which rarely results from the common method of digging holes.

We have now partially under our care, a pear orchard of upwards of one thousand dwarf and standard trees, planted shallow and well mulched, one year ago, according to our advice and direction, without a particle of stable manure under or about them, with a loss of only two trees in a thousand; and a finer pear orchard, of the same age and size, we feel assured, has never been seen in Pennsylvania. When this orchard gets into bearing, we intend to give a full description of our entire system of planting, manuring and pruning. We have, this fall, planted in this same orchard, nearly three thousand more pear trees, as shallow as possible, in no instance thrusting the spade, in digging the holes for them, into the sub-soil. The field has been thoroughly subsoiled, but not trenched or underdrained. The soil is, however, a good one, and the subsoil is gravelly and porous.

As to the propriety, and even necessity, of shallow planting in setting out trees, in all cases, to insure the

APPENDIX.

highest degree of success, we have no particle of doubt. We believe it is the only true and natural method.

And now, my dear amateur fruit grower, if you have a poor, sickly, unthrifty tree, deeply planted, which looks stunted and blighty, let me beg of you to try an experiment with it:—just dig the unfortunate tree out of the cold, rank grave in which you planted it, at once; lift it up gently with a large ball of earth attached to its roots, and place it on the good, warm, sweet surface soil, in a cavity which you can make with your foot, say two inches deep; throw around it a little good loam, mound up to it, and mulch it heavily, cut back the top freely in proportion to the loss of roots, and our word for it, you will see a change in the health and fruitfulness of your tree, in a few months, which will delight and astonish you.

Sub-soil ploughing, shallow planting, heavy mulching and surface manuring are the cardinal points in fruit culture. Under-draining may sometimes be necessary in heavy, wet soils, but with shallow planting, this expense, and also that of trenching, may be often avoided.

The editor of the *Gardener's Monthly* added the following note:—

"We believe one of the first, if not the very first article we ever wrote, at the suggestion of Mr. A. J. Downing, for his 'Horticulturist,' many years ago, was on the same subject, and presenting similar views as we have now the pleasure of inserting from the pen of Mr. Bright, and it is therefore needless to say how cordially we agree with him. We are at all times pleased to hear from Mr. Bright on any subject."

New method of Constructing Vineries

DETACHED AND DIVIDED BORDERS, ENTIRELY INSIDE THE HOUSE.

BY WILLIAM BRIGHT.

We have for a long time been of opinion that the common method of constructing vineries, with the border partly outside of the house, was not only unnecessary but absolutely injurious to the health and fruiting capacity of the vines. The success which we have attained in growing grapes in eleven inch pots, producing a large crop of the finest fruit without allowing the roots to extend beyond the limits of the pot, convinced us that borders of the size usually made were quite unnecessary. A moment's reflection upon the position of a vine, with part of its roots and all its wood in a hot-house, and its main roots out of doors, would suffice to impress any one at all familiar with grape culture, with the evident absurdity of the practice. Those who have had any experience in the matter, know how much we are at the mercy of the elements when vines are so planted, how little we can control the heat or moisture of the border, and what sad attacks the frost makes upon the roots of the vines after all our care in mulching, &c.

To break away from a custom, so hoary and reverend as this, is almost impossible; but we determined to do it, and now present for the consideration of gardeners a vinery constructed with the border not only entirely inside the house, but detached from the front wall by an air chamber four inches wide, separated also from the bottom soil by concrete and air chambers, and from the earth inside the house by similar air chambers, and then divided into sections two feet wide by brick work, so that the roots of one vine cannot mingle with the others, but each must remain as separate and distinct as if grown in a pot. This we call a detached and divided inside border, and we might add a suspended border, also, for the border is absolutely suspended in air, and nowhere do the sides of the border touch the adjacent soil or wall of the house. Under this arrangement, we attain a perfect drainage, and have entire control over the temperature and moisture of the border, and we think it will work admirably in practice.

We have just built a cold vinery on this plan, one hundred feet long, with a fixed roof, and a new method of ventilation, by means of numerous front and back shutters, which in our vanity we are pleased to think is a model of cheapness, beauty, and efficient working capacity. The house is a lean-to, seventeen feet wide, built in the best manner, and cost, with a back wall of concrete, sixteen inches thick, solid as stone, only about $450.

Without illustrations we can scarcely give a working plan of the house, but we may present such a description of the border as will serve to convey a pretty good idea of it.

The box or pit, into which the soil is placed, is constructed of brick-work, resting upon a concrete bottom. This concrete bottom is so bevelled as to throw the drainage into a channel constructed on one side, to carry off excess of water. Bricks are then set on edge, eight and a half inches apart, running in lines from the front of the house towards the back, and commencing four inches from the front wall, forming a set of piers, as it were, for the bottom of the pit to rest upon, and also forming tubes, or air chambers under the pit, for air to pass freely. The bottom of the pit is now laid with dry brick-work upon these lines or piers of brick, set on edge, being just the length of one brick apart. As soon as the bottom of the pit was thus laid, we built a wall of brick four inches thick, (the width of one brick,) four inches from the front wall of the house, to the height of two feet. We then divided the pit into sections of two feet, by erecting walls of brick set on edge, from the front to the back of the pit, of the same height as the front wall, making fifty sections or divisions in one hundred feet. After this, we finished the inside of the pit with boards, leaving a passage of four inches open to the air chambers below, so that the atmosphere of the house may circulate entirely under the border without obstruction.

. This completes the detached and divided border. It consists, in fact, of a huge brick pit, separated from the front, bottom, and inside of the house by air chambers four inches wide, and divided into sections, or large pots or tubs, by brick walls. Each section or division is two feet wide, three feet long, and two feet deep, and will contain soil enough to grow and fruit a vine fifteen feet long, (with the addition of manures and special fertilizers, by top-dressing,) for many years.

Now what are the advantages of such a border? We answer, the roots of the vines are placed entirely beyond the reach of frost and rain; and we have the most perfect control over the temperature and moisture of the whole border, at top and bottom. The border does not even touch the front wall of the house, which in cold weather must be a constant conductor of heat away from the border, doing immense mischief, especially in a forcing house. We can keep the border perfectly dry as long as we please in the spring, and we can dry it off as soon and as completely as we please in the fall. The bottom of the border must always have an atmosphere about it of the same temperature as the top-soil, or nearly so. We avoid the expense and care of a large border, which we are convinced is not only entirely unnecessary, but often highly injurious to the health and fruitfulness of the vines.

Again, with regard to the divisions into sections or

large pots, we can discover numerous and important advantages. It enables us to grow, in immediate proximity, vines of different degrees of vigor, which cannot be so grown in a common border, where the roots mingle together, without injury to the weaker kinds. It gives us an opportunity to water or to stimulate one vine without affecting another, or to withhold water from one without diminishing the growth of its neighbor. It permits us to try experiments with different fertilizing agents on single vines, and thus much may be learned, by comparison, of the value of different fertilizers, which cannot be done in a common border, with the same ease and precision. In the divided border, we can take out and put in vines at pleasure, without injury to the roots of other vines, and without breaking up a large portion of the border. If any vine proves too weak, or of a poor quality, we may remove it at once, and replace it with another vine of a better character, with the greatest ease, and the young vine so introduced, having a section of the pit all to itself, will receive no check from the roots of other vines. This is an important advantage. There is no reason why we should be so much hampered by the impossibility of changing the stock of a vinery, without grafting, inarching, &c. By the plan here described, all this difficulty is avoided, and we may change the vines in a house, as easily as we change the stock in our pots; removing unprofitable vines, and substituting fresh ones, well grown, from pots, ready for fruiting in a single year, whenever we choose, without difficulty, or without injury to the balance of the house.

This border, you will say, remains to be tried. This is true; but if we can fruit a vine with success and profit in an eleven inch pot, containing only about half a cubic foot of soil, can we not fruit a longer cane as successfully in twelve or fifteen cubic feet of soil, in the detached border?

Then, again, this border may easily be extended, if found necessary, to six feet or more long, with very little trouble and expense, though we doubt whether this will be required for many years. Or, the border may be made wider at first. But we think we prefer to have the inside of the house for other purposes, (at least for a year or two,) say for a propagating bed, or for a row of figs, or anything else you please. We shall of course expect to top-dress the border very freely with liquid manure, and special fertilizers; and we much prefer this method of growing grapes, where every part of the culture is under perfect control, to having large, cumbrous, sodden, sour, useless borders, exposed to rain and frost, over which we have little or no control.

The house in question, which we have just completed, is somewhat new in its construction, in other respects than those alluded to. It is set upon a terrace two feet high, to prevent it from looking too low, but the front sash and ventilator is only eighteen inches wide, and hence the roof is brought within two feet of the border, and the house is nowhere more than six feet and a half high, and has such a pitch to the roof that the grapes, when formed, must hang down, inside of the house, under and clear of the foliage, which, we think, adds much to the beauty of the sight which a house in full fruiting condition exhibits to the spectator.

INDEX.

	PAGE
Outline of Bright's Dwarf System of Grape Culture,	5
Culture of the Grape in Pots,	12
Propagation and Fruiting of Grapes in Pots,	18
Grape Culture in Gardens and Vineyards,	31
Preparation of Vineyard Soil,	33
Planting and Pruning Vineyards,	35
Mulching Vineyards,	42
Vines in City Yards,	46
Vines on Arbors,	47
Renewing Old Vines,	50
Ohio German System of Grape Culture,	52
Management of the Cold Vinery,	55
Atmospheric Conductors in Cold Vinery,	57
Inside and Divided Borders in Vinery,	59
Composts and Soils for Borders,	65
Planting and Training in Cold Vinery,	67
Management of Hot House,	73
Injurious Effects of Deep, Rich Borders, and Deep Planting in Vineyards,	74
Special Manures for the Grape,	81
Method of Applying the Fertilizer,	89

APPENDIX.

Inside Borders and Shallow Planting,	93
Shallow Planting of Trees,	106
New Method of Constructing Vineries,	115

www.ingramcontent.com/pod-product-compliance
Lightning Source LLC
Chambersburg PA
CBHW022140160426
43197CB00009B/1373